I0569932

NOT WHAT

SHIPS ARE

BUILT FOR

also by
STEVE ARNOLD

*INSPIRATION FROM A DOCTOR'S
REFLECTIONS ON LIFE, LOSS AND
THE AMERICAN HEALTH CARE
SYSTEM*

At times funny, at others, poignant, *Failure Is Only A Bruise* is an insider's observations on working in the medical malpractice field, with frank and painfully honest insights on everything from the inner workings of the 'Medical-Industrial-Political Machine' to coping with the fallout of bad decisions—an invaluable resource and inspiration for everyone 'going through it'.

"... *A compelling narrative that is both informative and inspiring... a testament to resilience in the face of adversity and a reminder that even in the midst of failures, there is always an opportunity for growth and healing.*" —Brandon Drabek, ND

Available now on
amazon

NOT WHAT SHIPS ARE BUILT FOR

A VIEW FROM THE EDGE

By

Steve Arnold

Chardon, Ohio, USA

Taylor & Wells Publishing
11525 Taylor-Wells Rd.
Chardon, OH, USA 44024
www.taylor-wells.com

First Print Edition

Copyright © 2024 by Steve Arnold

All rights reserved. No part of this publication may be reproduced, distributed, or transmitted in any form or by any means, including photocopying, recording, or other electronic or mechanical methods, without the prior written permission of the author, except in the case of brief quotations embodied in critical reviews and certain other noncommercial uses permitted by copyright law.

Front cover illustration: *Study for the Voyage Of Life: Manhood*, by Thomas Cole, 1839

Printed in the United States of America

ISBN 979-8-9908505-6-9

FOR CHRIS AND BRIAN.
WHO SAT BY ME IN CHURCH WHEN
OTHERS WOULDN'T.

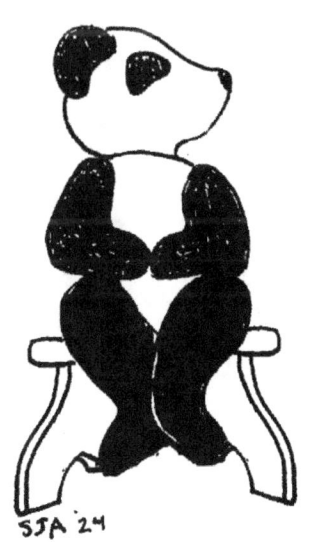

Table of Contents

Shake Well Before Opening

'And it came to pass that the Lord commanded me, wherefore I did make plates of ore that I might engraven upon them the record of my people.'

—1 Nephi 19:1

Life is rough. Painful. Scary. Often unjust. Does it *have* to be this way? Is this really what I came here for?

I've been a member of the Church of Jesus Christ of Latter-day Saints for over twenty years. Despite what you may think from the youthful vigor apparent in my photo (!), I joined in my middle-age years, after a long and meandering journey peeking in at many other religions. I had lived an entire lifetime as an agnostic before that day in May 2002. The exact path that brought me to this place is not

one I want to share here (it's very personal to me) but suffice it to say that this was the first church in which I really *felt* something. That, at least, got me to start investigating the Church to see what it was all about. Once I started that, I began finding answers to questions I hadn't even realized I had. Gaps in the understanding of what some would call 'mainstream' Christianity began getting filled in. Apparent inconsistencies in doctrines were reconciled. I found then, and still do, that this church *makes sense* to me.

The purpose of this book is to explore some of those things I've learned, both at the onset, and in the decades since. I'm writing from the perspective of a member of the Church so you may find references to scriptures and people unfamiliar to you, like the quote at the start of this chapter. Don't let that put you off! There's a lot of commonality in our attitudes, and I wrote this because I'm confident the meanings will be clear. And you can always get a free copy of the LDS scriptures and read it for yourself—a tactic I strongly encourage. Just so you know, the LDS Church canon counts these as 'The Standard Works':

The Old Testament
The New Testament
The Book of Mormon

The Doctrine and Covenants
The Pearl of Great Price

For the Bible we only use the King James Version, believing it to be the closest to the original Hebrew, Greek and Aramaic. All of these books carry a similar weight for us, and each has its particular strengths for certain topics. If you're curious, I'd be willing to discuss! Just drop me an email at sjarnoldcreative@gmx.com. Or go to LDS.org.

Now, full disclosure: I'm not going to lie to you and tell you that I'm a model church member, or that I haven't made my fair share of mistakes (or even more so). I have indeed had my ups and downs. At times I've been right on the line, and at others I've been right on the edge. Times I've felt like Moroni (the second one, a prophet and military leader of his people) and others I've felt like Omni, who was given charge of sacred records and rather boldly declared (in writing, mind you):

> 'Wherefore, in my days, I would that ye should know that I fought much with the sword to preserve my people, the Nephites, from falling into the hands of their enemies, the Lamanites. But behold, I of myself am a

wicked man, and I have not kept the statutes and the commandments of the Lord as I ought to have done.

... I had kept these plates [i.e., the records] according to the commandments of my fathers; and I conferred them upon my son Amaron.'

—Book of Mormon

Omni 1: 2-3

Despite his self-declared faults Omni knew the value of passing on learning that came his way. It didn't matter if it came from his own life or from those who had come before.

That's pretty much what I'm doing. In those times I'm toeing the line I can see the amazing possibilities awaiting on the other side of the Veil; but the view from the edge shows me just how far some of us have yet to come, and even why some (much to the utter confusion of most members in the Church) may choose not to cross that distance at all.

In Part One I look at some of the workings of our doctrine. There's no particular significance to the topics I've selected, hence the title which references that old coffee

can of random fasteners my Grandpa used to keep in his garage. Part Two is more about *being* a member of the Church, and not just taking part in the actions, but the topics are just as random.

I'm not writing this to try to convert anyone. These are just things I've learned that I feel are worth sharing that can be an encouragement to everyone, LDS or not. We're *all* still learning, after all. If you're not a member of the Church, remember that these are my observations, not necessarily official Church doctrine (though I try to be as close as my understanding allows). If you are a member some of this will be familiar territory, but maybe you will find something here you hadn't considered in the past. In either case I sincerely hope I can leave something of worth to you.

Steve Arnold
Chardon, Ohio
June 2024

PART ONE

A Can Of
Nuts & Bolts

It Is
The Doom Of Men
That They Forget

'And a book of remembrance was kept, in the which was recorded, in the language of Adam, for it was given unto as many as called upon God to write by the spirit of inspiration.'

—Moses 6:5

I like movies. Movies like *Raiders of the Lost Ark*, *Sky Captain and The World Of Tomorrow*, or *Who Framed Roger Rabbit*—which I don't want to admit how excited I was when I found it on DVD. Or my perennial favorite, *Big Trouble in Little China*.

Obviously, these are adventure movies, and pretty cheesy ones. Not the kind of fare that typically lends itself

to deep thinking. But every once in a while, I find that the writer has—it would seem almost unwittingly—slipped in a line that turns out to be very profound.

All the way back in 1981 Orion Pictures released *Excalibur.* Of course it was about King Arthur and Merlin and all the Knights of the Round Table (what else could it be?). I thought the movie was okay, for the most part, but there was one line that struck me when I first saw the film and has remained with me ever since: following the Britons' victory at Badon, Merlin gives the Round Table Gang a very Henry V-esque speech in which he admonishes them to remember the battle and re-tell the story often because '… it is the doom of men that they forget'.

I have found in my life that this is painfully true. Our attention span as a culture is famous for being embarrassingly short. Wars break out, soldiers get deployed, people die and destruction rains down—but within weeks the news cycle is overtaken by some random viral social media sensation. And only days later they, in turn, will be supplanted by something even more insipid. Media pundits themselves complain about our lack of attentiveness while hurriedly urging us to focus on the next Big Crisis. But I don't believe we have a monopoly on this

doom, or that we came up with it first. I seem to recall a book (I'm sure you've heard of it, if you're LDS [wink wink nudge nudge]) about a people that went through cycles of piety and sinfulness: at first righteous and filled with spiritual fervor, then within a generation awash in greed and decadence; first caring for their fellow man, then despising him, over and over again, until they met their end in a retribution visited upon them by their own kin sixteen centuries ago. They never seemed to remember the painful lessons of their past. They always insisted on repeating the same mistakes, as if each succeeding generation felt they were somehow 'different' or 'superior' or 'more learned', or that 'circumstances had changed'. Or simply that the old rules were just out of date and no longer relevant.

This forgetfulness, this arrogance, is why Adam was told to keep a Book Of Remembrance. This is why 2 Chronicles when the priest Hilkiah stumbled upon a copy of Moses' Book of the Law while cleaning out Solomon's Temple after years of neglect, he read it to King Josiah of Judah who 'rent his clothes' for the realization of how far they had drifted from their original faith. This is why we are encouraged to keep journals. This is why we are told in Doctrine & Covenants Section 20 that 'it is expedient that the church meet together often to partake of bread and wine in the remembrance of the Lord Jesus'.

In the LDS church we take the sacrament every week. Now I should confess that when I sat in on other churches' services over the years, I never actually went to any one church more than once—none of them ever impressed me that much. But I was really surprised to learn later on that most other churches don't do a sacrament service more than maybe once a month, if that. Perhaps that was one of the reasons I felt this was the right place, because it seems instinctive to me that this is something that should be done every chance one has. Because, well... it is the doom of men that they forget.

But all that aside, some may wonder why we *do* do this every week. First of all, let's look at the promises made: We believe the sacrament is a renewal of our baptismal covenant. We promise, in taking the bread, to demonstrate our willingness to be called by his name, to *remember* him, and keep his commandments, and in exchange for this we are promised to have his Spirit accompany us. We promise in taking the water again to *remember* him, and again in exchange we receive the promise of the company of his Spirit. (As for why it's water now instead of wine, read on). This is the same exchange of promises when we are

interviewed for our baptism and afterwards confirmed a member. The message is pretty clear: we need to remember. We need to remember what we have been taught, and what we believe, and who we are. We have to be reminded frequently, because it is a tough world, full of distractions and diversions, and... it is the doom of men that they forget.

In the Book of Mormon there is a very vivid description of a dream by a prophet named Lehi, in 1 Nephi Chapter 8. As it was shown in Lehi's dream,

> '...there arose a mist of darkness . . . insomuch that they who had commenced on the path did lose their way, that they wandered off and were lost. And it came to pass that I beheld others pressing forward, and they came forth and caught hold of the rod of iron, and they did press forward through the mist of darkness, clinging to the rod of iron, even until they did come forth and partake of the fruit of the tree.'
>
> —1 Nephi 8:23-24

The tree was the Tree of Life, and the 'iron rod' represented the writings left to us to guide us there.

Now imagine that you are lost in darkness—and you have a lifeline to which you cling. I once watched a documentary about dust storms in the Plains during the Great Depression, how they were called 'black blizzards' and how farmers would have to tie a rope from the house to the barn so they could find their way back and forth in the choking grit carried on seventy-mile-an-hour winds. I was amazed how easy it would have been to lose one's way and wander off into the wastes if one did not hold on tight—possibly to perish in the storm. The only way to stay on course was to keep a close hold on the rope.

These times are the same. The storms rage about us, trying to blow us off the path, to make us let go of that guideline and to raise the dust so thick about us that we cannot see where our next step should fall. But we must keep a close hold. We must go hand over hand as it were, clinging to that guide from one sacrament to the next, in order to stay on course so we can make it back from this cold and drafty barn we call the terrestrial world to the warmth and safety of our Father's house. In the Dust Bowl, to let go—even for a few steps—during one of these black blizzards was to invite distraction, disorientation, and possibly even destruction, and the risks are just as real today; the winds just as strong, the obscuring dust just as thick.

The symbolism of the sacrament is very simple. Bread and water, solid and liquid, to remind us how Jesus' body was beaten and his blood was spilled for us as the ultimate stand-in for the most essential ordinance of atonement, where he took that punishment 'for and in behalf of (fill in your name)'.

We started out using bread and wine, at first. But there was a problem not long after the Church's founding of ensuring the wine bought for the purpose wasn't somehow tainted (spell that p-o-i-s-o-n-e-d) by those who wished us ill (and if you think that's dramatic, you should read about some of the persecutions back then). Since then, we've been told it really doesn't matter what we use for the sacrament. We don't believe it turns into a literal blood and body. It's just a memory jogger. It's like taking the red pill in the Matrix, it's an outward sign of your inner intentions. It could be crackers and Kool-Aid if that was all you had:

> '. . . it mattereth not what ye shall eat or what ye shall drink when ye partake of the sacrament, if it so be that ye do it with an eye single to my glory—*remembering* unto the Father my body which was laid down for you, and my blood which was shed for the

remission of your sins.'

—Doctrine & Covenants 27:2

The bread and water are like variables in a math equation. It makes no difference from what alphabet you draw your letters, x, y, and z or α, β, and γ. What matters is only that you all agree on what each represents.

The sacrament is the core of our worship service. Its regular observance is one of those habits that sets us apart from other churches, and I feel for good reason. I can testify that I have survived many difficult times just by hanging on from one sacrament meeting to another, pulling myself along, hand over hand, clinging to the lifeline in the dust storm. I know that there have also been many times that I have missed a sacrament meeting due to my work schedule, illness, lack of motivation or whatever, and my week suffered for the lack of it. Truly it can be difficult at times to get up early, get dressed, and make it in to church, but I know I need the refresher. I need the reminder, for I have seen that 'it is the doom of men that they forget', and my memory is stretched enough already.

Shedding The Millstone

'For with God nothing shall be impossible.'
—Luke 1:37

Addiction. To be uncontrollably dependent upon something detrimental to your health. A thousand different ways to lose control of your life. Reams of paper have been printed in our church, and many others, to urge their people to stay out of addiction's grip.

On the other side of the line an entire industry exists to help those in recovery. And yet relapses are common, so much so that for an addict in rehab, every anniversary, be it week, month, year, or decade, is justifiably worth celebrating.

In this moment I'm not speaking to those shying away from the edge. Nor am I writing to those who have trod

this path many times before. All of those folks are in familiar (though not necessarily comfortable) territory.

Right now, I want to speak to those who've just crossed that line. To the ones who have just found themselves in that prison. Because your question, I am sure, is not so much 'Where did I go wrong?'. We all have 20/20 hindsight and usually we can look back and see exactly where we made our mistakes. You're probably rather wondering 'What do I do now?'. It's fine to know where you turned off the path, but that is of little help when you find yourself lost deep in the forest. You need to get yourself out.

And that's not necessarily very easy to do. Finding the path is one thing, but embarking upon it and staying with it are something entirely separate. As a doctor I can prescribe all kinds of medicines to help you deal with the physical cravings of things you're hooked on. I can give you nicotine patches, Antabuse and Chantix. I can steer you toward a rehab center and support groups. Within the Church we have addiction recovery programs for pretty much anything you deal with. All these things can be done for you.

But the last little bit of it has to come from within you. You have to take that last step back over the line to sobriety and there is nothing I can give you, and no program in the Church or without, that can do that for you.

But how do you do that? How do you handle when the cravings come, sometimes years after you thought you were past it? And they will come. Alcoholics know this. You are never truly free. You must face every day, you must face every hour, ready for the challenge. You can never let your guard down. You can never, once you have put it behind you, allow any place for even a fleeting dalliance with the temptations. You cannot make, as Jeffrey R. Holland (one of our apostles) once put it, a 'place in your heart for the enemy of your soul'.

When those moments happen, you must occupy your heart and mind with other things. When you feel the pull of old habits you must turn your attention instead toward some other focus, something that will uplift you. Something that will draw you into the light and not away from it. It doesn't have to be religion, if you're not up for that, though that's a good place to start. But don't worry— the rush of a craving is just that, it's a rush. It is over almost as quickly as it comes. If you can hold out only for even a

few minutes, quite often that will make all the difference. Yes, you will have to fight that battle again in an hour, or a day, or a month, but you will have gotten through that episode, and that's one less time you gave in. And you will find with time that every time you step away, it will get a little easier to do. Though it never really goes away, it will get more manageable.

I mentioned that there is nothing the medical community can give you to help you take that last step over the line. But that does not mean you have to take that step completely alone. Addictions are the stuff of stealth and shadows. They exemplify the shame that keeps us away from the light of God and makes us slink away into 'Outer Darkness'. It causes us to look upon our own selves, clad in soiled garments, loathing what we have done with ourselves. But we need not spend the remainder of our existence in such gloom. Lorenzo Snow, fifth president of the LDS church, said: 'The Lord has not given us the gospel that we may go around mourning all the days of our lives.'

During the April 2006 LDS General Conference Elder Joseph B. Wirthlin gave a talk about 'The Abundant Life'. In it he said:

'Do you seek peace of mind? ... Forgiveness? ...
Drink deeply of living waters.... Too many sit
at the banquet table of the Gospel... and
merely nibble at the feast placed before them.
They go through the motions—attending
their meetings perhaps, glancing at scriptures,
repeating familiar prayers—but their hearts
are far away.... We are sons and daughters of
an immortal, loving, and all-powerful Father
in Heaven.'

I want you to pay particular attention to his next
statement:

'We are created as much from the dust of
eternity as we are from the dust of the earth.
Every one of us has a potential we can scarcely
imagine.'

His remarks may feel as though they are directed at
Church members, but they really apply to everyone. You
very likely will need help, and you will need the Holy Ghost.
And you can't get that help just by dropping to the ground
and waiting. If you want out of the woods, *you* must locate
the path. *You* must follow it out. *You* must stay on it. But

luckily there are people already on that path calling to you. As with the leprous Syrian general Naaman seeking a cure for *his* afflictions, it really can be as simple as bathing in the river Jordan, but *you are the one who has got to get into the water*—all the way in, over and over again.

I have heard it said that God will not test you more than you can bear. *This is not true*, and is a distortion by well-meaning people. He will not *tempt* you more than you can bear (see 1 Corinthians 10:13), but he will certainly *test* you beyond your ability. This is to teach you to have the humility to ask for help. For we bystanders also are commanded to help our fellow man, and how can we do that, if our neighbors are not tested to the point of needing help? We all must take our turns at some point as an injured traveler so that others can be the Good Samaritans. We are expected to ask for help. Accept the fact that you need it and seek it out.

The hosts of heaven stand by waiting to aid us, and to assist those around us trying to help us. But why do they stand by? Why *don't* they just jump in at the first sign of trouble? Why allow us to get into these fixes in the first place? Because we need some skin in the game. Because quite often we won't admit to ourselves that we need the

help until we've slid a long way down that slippery slope. We have to recognize for ourselves that we are in over our heads. There's little in this world so futile as trying to help someone who doesn't realize they are in trouble (ask any professional who deals with addiction about the 'pre-contemplative' stage). So, pay attention to yourself and recognize where you are. It's better for you if you make that assessment for yourself, now, than wait until you are standing before the Judgment Bar of God and have it pointed out to you. I am pretty sure there will be many empty apologies made there. You don't want yours to be one of them.

I firmly believe there was a reason Jesus was born into the house of Joseph. He was not born into wealth, or honor, or status, but likewise neither was he born into abject poverty. The manger was temporary. Joseph obviously had the money to get a room. No, Jesus was born into the house of a carpenter so that as a child he would grow up at the elbow of his earthly father, learning how to take natural wood, rough and green, and cure it, age it, shape it, smooth it and make it beautiful, and assemble it into something functional. Doesn't that sound familiar? And then when things would break, he would learn how to mend them and put their fractured pieces back together.

What about timing? Is it too late? Absolutely not, and I can say that with confidence even though I don't know what you're dealing with. It has been well established that one of the favorite tactics the Adversary uses on us is to make us think we have gone too far. That there is no redemption available to us, for we have sinned too long and too often.

Well, forget that. God has made it abundantly clear it makes no difference how far down those dark paths you've gone, he will still bring you back. God is waiting to forgive you, and if he is willing to do that, *who are you to argue with him?* Admit your mistake, learn your lesson, turn away from your errors, forgive yourself, and ask God for help.

But do it now. Just because you can be redeemed at any point does not mean how far you've gone makes no difference to *you*. Every step taken in the wrong direction is still a step you must retrace. Every day spent in the weeds is a day of joy lost to you never to be regained. And it *is* possible to go so far that, even though he can still pull *you* back, you may end up losing more along the way than you can bear. So, while it is true God can accept your redemption almost anywhere along the way, it's easier for both of you if you start now. Right now. Today. Do not

procrastinate the day of your salvation. Do not allow the Adversary to gently wrap his golden chains around you and lead you any further down that broad avenue to Hell. Take control of your life at this moment and make this the day that you get up on your feet.

If you need help, get it! Whether you struggle with pornography, tobacco, alcohol, drugs, forgiveness of your fellow man or forgiveness of yourself, know you do not face your demons alone. There is hope and help standing by for you. And do not doubt that it will be there. Do not judge yourself unworthy. Do not fear that you, with the Lord's help, will be unequal to the task. As Dieter Uchtdorf, another one of our current apostles, said once, 'Do not doubt your faith. Doubt your fears!'

You do not have to swim in the deep end alone. And if you find yourself floundering there, don't panic—after all, your lifeguard walks on water. He can help you shed that millstone that is hanging around your neck.

Wherever you are, wherever you have been, there is a lifeline provided for you. And it's not just a twisty rope so slick with your own tears that you can't hold on. It is a rod of iron, firmly anchored and brightly polished by the firm

grip of so many thousands who have walked this road before you. Take hold of it. And once you've done that, reach back and take the hand of another and bring them to it. It's easier to stand if there are two of you! And then you both hold on, together.

And if that's all you can do, if you lack the strength to advance even one more step, then the two of you stay put, dig in your heels and hold on for all you're worth:

> 'What man of you, having an hundred sheep, if he lose one of them, doth not leave the ninety and nine in the wilderness and go after that which is lost, until he find it?
> And when he hath found it, he layeth it on his shoulders, rejoicing.
> And when he cometh home, he calleth together his friends and neighbours, saying uno them, Rejoice with me; for I have found my sheep which was lost.'
>
> —Luke 15:4-6

Be not afraid, little lost lamb. Someone will find you.

The Holy Ghost

'But he, being full of the Holy Ghost, looked up steadfastly into heaven, and saw the glory of God, and Jesus standing on the right hand of God.'

—Acts 7: 55

One of the biggest differences between the Church of Jesus Christ of Latter-day Saints and most other Christian denominations is our understanding of the Godhead, what most others call the Trinity: the three-part government of God, Jesus, and the Holy Ghost. The understanding that's been given us is that these three entities are separate personages. This makes sense, when you read the account of Stephen in Acts Chapter 7 who actually saw God and Jesus standing side-by-side. How the Trinity as a concept came about also makes sense to me (in a rather cynical way, I am going to apologize now for) when

you study the goings-on of the Council at Nicea. Still, my understanding of the current take on the Trinity in other churches is that they are one 'nature', and three 'persons'. This is not very far off from the LDS teachings where these three personages are 'one' in the sense of being *completely united in purpose and intent.*

This notion of three-part authority is a common theme in the leadership structure of the LDS Church: the ward bishop has two counselors, as do his auxiliary organization leaders like those running the Elders' Quorums, the youth sections, and others. Even the president of the entire Church, the Prophet, has them. Within that triumvirate each will have specific tasks to handle so that not every duty devolves onto the leader's shoulders alone.

In this sense we see the Holy Ghost as one of God's counselors and as having a particular role to play. He is a being of spirit, as opposed to God and Jesus Christ, for as it is necessary that they have physical bodies in order to create the world and bestow priesthood keys, so it is necessary for the Holy Ghost to be spirit only, so he can speak to all.

This, in particular, is his charge—to bear witness of God. To light your soul with the sure knowledge of eternal truths, to manifest to each of us the reality of the World; not this shallow, venal shell that we can perceive with five limited senses, but the true nature of things and our place in an eternal existence. To confirm to those seeking the path that they have indeed found it; to encourage the new traveler that they yet remain on the way, and to strengthen the weary veteran of the spiritual wars that hope and help is ready at hand.

There are two aspects to the Holy Ghost: his *power* and his *gift*. By the *power* of the Holy Ghost our natural consciousness is brought to an awareness of our state and the amazing alternative available to us. For this the Holy Ghost speaks to all who will listen. In fact, we are told that, once we (as one not a member, looking into the Church) have read the Book of Mormon, we need ask the Holy Ghost if it is true. Getting a confirming response actually needs to happen *before* we are baptized. And to the Church members: should you ever doubt that the Holy Ghost speaks to all, remember this story where Peter was preaching to a crowd of Gentiles:

'While Peter yet spake these words, the Holy

Ghost fell on all them which heard the word.
And they of the circumcision which believed
were astonished, as many as came with Peter,
because that on the Gentiles also was poured
out the gift of the Holy Ghost.
For they heard them speak with tongues, and
magnify God. Then answered Peter,
Can any man forbid water, that these should
not be baptized, which have received the Holy
Ghost as well as we?'

— Acts 10:44-47

In contrast to the power of the Holy Ghost, the *gift* of the Holy Ghost is given to you after baptism, you're your confirmation. With this you are entitled to have the Holy Ghost as your constant companion. He will be a guide to you, helping you stay out of trouble (if you listen!), directing you to a better, richer life. Not necessarily an easier or more prosperous life, for the Holy Ghost does not deal with the petty attractions of this world, but with eternal riches that are much more worthwhile—strength of character, understanding of complex things, and probably most importantly, peace of mind in troubled times. This is the same guidance available to all in the Church right up to

and including the Prophet. Without it we would be nothing more than a Bible study group. Brigham Young, second president of the Church, once said,

> 'Without this privilege in the Gospel,
> connected with the gifts of the Holy Ghost, I
> should be inclined to believe that the religion
> that is taught in the Bible and in the Book of
> Mormon, would amount to nothing more
> than a mere phantom—an imaginary thing. It
> would be inadequate to satisfy, in any degree,
> the mind of man, as it is now organized.'

How valuable is this? It won't buy you a car, or a house, or even an iPad. But it can direct the desperate to necessities of life in times of need, and things which will be of much use to you both on earth and in heaven. I will close this chapter with the words of Wilford Woodruff, fourth president of the Church:

> 'You may surround any man or woman with
> all the wealth and glory that the imagination
> of man can grasp, and are they satisfied? No.
> There is still an aching void. On the other
> hand, show me a beggar upon the streets, who

has the Holy Ghost, whose mind is filled with that spirit and power, and I will show you a person who has peace of mind, who possesses true riches, and those enjoyments that no man can obtain from any other source. The servants of God, in every age of the world, have been sustained and nerved up to do their duty by this power; and I will say to the Latter-day Saints, if they will be faithful, and do what they should do, and listen to the counsel given to them, they need not have any fears about anything, for the whole work is in the hands of God, the destinies of nations lie there.'

The Sacrifices of Jesus

'For it is expedient that there should be a great and last sacrifice; yea, not a sacrifice of man, neither of beast... but it must be an infinite and eternal sacrifice.'

—Alma 34:10

Not gonna lie, there has been a *world* of trouble these last several years. Pandemic. Saber-rattling, or even outright war. Civil unrest. Bitter political battles that have strained otherwise solid relationships. These have weighed heavily upon most of us in one way or another. Folks have lost income, or jobs altogether. Some have lost their health, a place to live, or cherished friends, family, or colleagues. Some have felt that even their God has forgotten them.

At the LDS General Conference in October 2008 Elder Quentin L. Cook (*another* one of our apostles) gave a talk that is as relevant today as it was then. He called it 'Hope Ya Know, We Had A Hard Time'. It was later made

into a short video now available online and remains one of my favorite talks of all time. Elder Cook's ultimate point was:

> 'I testify that the Atonement of Jesus Christ covers all of the hardships that any of us will encounter in this life. At times when we may feel to say, 'Hope you know, I had a hard time', we can be assured that he is there and we are safe in his loving arms.'

But at times like these, in the midst of sore trials, we may be inclined to doubt that the Lord really knows. We may *know* that he knows, but do we *feel and believe* that he does? Is he sensitive to the sacrifices we are making?

To that end I wanted to take some space to talk about the sacrifices Jesus made in the course of his mortal life. Of course, we all know of, and often study in detail, the Atonement. But I'm referring to other hardships he went through. I started out making a list, and by the time I got done it was quite long:

There is the fact he almost didn't have a father. Joseph was going to quietly divorce Mary when she was found to be carrying Jesus, until an angel implored him to stay.

There was the flight to Egypt to escape Herod. There was the trip from Nazareth to Jerusalem three times a year to attend feasts at the temple. That was 90 miles, or about five days on foot or donkey-back, each way, each time (if you're interested in that sort of thing, take a look at orbis.stanford.edu, a website that calculates travel times and costs across the Roman Empire [and yes, I'm that much of a geek that I have it bookmarked]). There was the *waiting*... he knew at the age of twelve what he had coming before him, yet he had to wait almost another twenty years before it finally started happening (while having to turn away from sin that entire time). There was serving his father as a young carpenter. Some of you may have had personal experience with what it means to listen to your dad all day at work, and then all night at home! There were the forty-day fasts. There was the constant being on the run, even after Herod was dead, of having to avoid the Romans and the Sanhedrin. There was the need to watch his mother watch him suffer...

That's quite an impressive list. I'm not going to look at all of these, but I did want to look at a few that we usually don't, or take a gander from a different angle than what we usually do.

Let's start with his youth. Jesus 'served his father'. Joseph was a carpenter, a tradesman. Joseph's family was not in the upper tier of society, living comfortably off investments and accumulated wealth. Nor were they at the bottom, begging in the streets and being dependent upon others' generosity (or lack of the same). We don't know if they were ineligible for the regular dole of wheat that characterized the Roman welfare system, but we have no real reason to expect they were. I think it's safe to assume they were squarely in the middle, working for a living, paying taxes, and carrying the load of society. Joseph, and by extension his sons, including Jesus, were expected to get up every day and go to work. They were expected to meet the needs of the customer. I was watching *The Chosen* on TV and there is a scene in one episode, prior to the start of his ministry, where he is fashioning a door latch. Could you imagine having a door latch made by Jesus? Could you imagine having to take it back because it wasn't working right?

But back to business: he's getting up every day and going to work because in those days, there was no salary. No 401k. No health insurance. No paid vacations. You didn't work, you didn't eat. I'd spent plenty of years punching a time clock and can attest to the fact that either

work is slow and you have the time to relax and enjoy your life, but no money to do so, or work is frantic and you have the money but no time. So his sacrifice there was having to spend most of his time trying to keep the business going, just surviving and not having much time to devote to anything else.

Then there was the learning. Obviously when he was born, he knew nothing. We can be pretty sure of this because he was specifically sent here to experience life as we did, and we have a veil drawn over our eyes when we get here. According to Norman W. Gardner in his essay "What We Know About Premortal Life", 'Our memory of premortal life has been withheld. This was necessary to help us to learn to walk by faith and prepare us to become like Him.'

Now it was tradition among the Jews of the time to begin a boy's education at the age of six with the reading and writing of scripture. At the age of twelve they would be taken to Jerusalem to pass their final exam. By the time Jesus reached this point he was teaching the scholars in the temple, not the other way around. He knew by that time that he was to 'be about my Father's business'. But it wasn't time for him to start his ministry then, so clearly there was

still a learning curve he was climbing:

> 'And I, John, saw that he received not of the
> fulness at the first, but received grace for grace,
> and he received not of the fulness at first, but
> continued from grace to grace, until he
> received a fulness; and thus he was called the
> Son of God, because he received not of the
> fulness at the first.'
>
> —Doctrine & Covenants 93:12-14

Now there's an interesting point to be made while we are in that scripture, that he received 'grace for grace', which I take to mean the more he demonstrated what he knew, the more knowledge he was given. That's a great life lesson about the workings of the Gospel.

So think on this: we have to go through life not knowing the plan in advance. This isn't an accident; it's set up that way so our faith can be tested. Your faith can't be tested if you already 'know' something, if you've already seen the proof. This is why Jesus Christ only reveals himself to those who already have great faith. He wants you to believe *because you choose to believe,* not because you are compelled to by physical proof. In the Book of Mormon,

38

Alma, a Nephite prophet, says this:

> 'Yea, there are many who do say: If thou wilt
> show unto us a sign from heaven, then we
> shall know of a surety; then we shall believe.
> Now I ask, is this faith? Behold, I say unto you,
> Nay; for if a man knoweth a thing he hath no
> cause to believe, for he knoweth it.'
>
> —Alma 32:17-18

So we go through life not really knowing what's coming for sure, but learning to have the faith that God knows what we need and will watch out for us. Still, though, it's nerve-wracking! It's tough being God's pointman.

For Jesus, I imagine it was the same way. He didn't know everything about who he was and where he was going, at least not all at once. He had to wait and learn a piece at a time, and when we're young, that's pretty hard. He had to experience enough of life's uncertainties to even have a context, to have a frame to hang his experiences on.

Next let's talk about how Jesus lost his father. Twice, in fact, when you think of it. First there was Joseph.

There's an old African expression that says 'You're not really a man until your father dies'. Those of you who have lost a parent, *any* parent figure to whom you were close and to whom you looked to as an example for yourself, can relate to this. I was raised by my grandfather and it's been decades since he passed away. That was a challenging time in my life for many reasons, but in the middle of everything else I suddenly realized I was the patriarch of the family. I would no longer be able to stop by my grandpa's house and ask him how to fix this or handle that, or just spend a little time taking in the house I grew up in. Suddenly it was on me. I like to think he prepared me well enough, but still, realizing there was no one standing behind me to back me up was a sobering thought.

We don't know when Joseph died. He was still present when Jesus was twelve and teaching at the temple, and hale and hearty enough to be frantically searching an entire city for him. But by the time Jesus was beginning his mortal ministry eighteen years later Joseph was gone. What about his character? We know that Mary was an exceptional person to have been chosen as Jesus' mother, but what can we surmise about Jospeh? We don't usually talk about him (there's not much information to discuss), but he must also have been special if he was entrusted with the Savior's early

years, those critical times before Jesus reached the age of six and started to learn the scriptures. He was entrusted with educating Jesus about right and wrong, duty, and compassion, all traits that Joseph lived. When Joseph found out Mary was carrying Jesus an angel convinced him not to divorce her. He knew that that no one was going to believe the story of her conception, yet he stayed. And that brings up the fact he was visited by angels. And don't forget the flight into Egypt. To pack up one's family and flee to another country is a daunting task. There was no guarantee they would ever return.

The second time Jesus lost his father was on the cross, when he had to be left alone by God at the very end. A moment that prompted the Lord to call out (and please forgive my paraphrasing), 'Papa, where are you? Why did you leave me?' As we study the Atonement we see that was a necessary part of the job description, but it can reassure us that the Lord knows in spades what it's like to be alone and bereft of those closest to you.

Then there was the turning away from sin. Jesus spent a lifetime avoiding and rejecting temptation. This is a challenge for most of us, and since we are imperfect, one we rarely meet. He had to put in a tremendous effort, at least

from the age of accountability (what we LDS believe is about eight years old), every *single* day (probably more often than that!).

But think of this: he didn't just turn down dessert, or decide to go to sabbath when he would rather have stayed in bed, or decided against going camel-tipping with his 'good-for-nothing friends'. He resisted the snappy comeback, the scathing critique, the back-biting and gossiping that so many people indulge in like they are trying for their third gold in the event. He turned away from pride. He was teaching in the temple at twelve, do you think he could have put the Pharisees in their place when he was thirty? He did, but in such a way that a thoughtful person would have felt good about it. He avoided sloth and prized hard work. Remember the parable of the talents? One guy had that which he was given taken away because he was lazy. Never mind that he was lazy because he was fearful, he was still lazy.

There's another sin not commonly listed in the classic 'top seven' list, known as 'acedia'; this is best defined as 'apathetic neglect'. Jesus wasn't known for this either. He stopped in the middle of a crowd to find a woman who had reached out to touch him. Several other times he dropped

what he was doing or changed course to answer a summons for help. It wasn't just a list of things he wasn't doing, there were things involving 'not doing' that he was actively countering.

Then there's the Atonement. There are hundreds, if not more, discussions on the Atonement, in talks and articles and books, and you can avail yourself of any of these for some really insightful contemplation. It has been said by most Christians the Atonement started on the Cross. In the LDS Church our understanding is that it started in the Garden of Gethsemane. I might offer that it began at the Grand Council in the pre-existence (more on *that* later) when the Plan of Salvation was proposed to all of us, and Jesus stepped forward to volunteer the infinite atonement. I think he probably had a pretty good idea at that moment what was coming, yet there he was.

There's one particular point that always gets a little bit of a gloss-over that I feel shouldn't: what exactly does it mean to suffer an 'infinite atonement'? I get the feeling listening to people talk (LDS and non -member alike) that they have the idea he somehow experienced some measurable quantity of suffering for everything we've done. Now all the things I've done, plus all the things done by

everyone I know, plus all the things done by everyone that has ever lived, seems to add up to an awful lot of suffering. A staggering amount of suffering, in fact, that I can't get my head around. In fact, I think that most people can't get their head around it, and I feel this maybe inclines us to put Jesus up on a pedestal the shape, size and scope of which we can't even conceive.

But as Lorenzo Snow said, 'As Man is, God once was; as God is, Man may become', and this applies to all his children—and Jesus was one of His children. This means we are more alike than we realize (I should say I'm elevating us more to God's level than vice versa). I would propose that the pain he suffered was in fact more along the lines of 'greater than any one pain anyone could have inflicted upon them'. That's still a lot of pain, and this particular thought is only the gospel according to Steve, so take it with a grain of salt, but for me thinking of it this way puts it into much more understandable terms.

It's still enough to cover anything you or I or anyone else will ever go through, but this way he isn't some kind of super-hero—unreachable, unattainable, and unlikely to notice us mere mortals. It makes him more of a brother, one that has been hurt worse than anything I could ever do

to myself. Not the kind of 'being' that will stand over me with his arms folded, saying 'You think you had it bad? Let me tell you what I've been through', but rather a loving and maybe a bit tragic sibling who still has the heart, when he sees me in pain, to put his arm around me and say 'I know what it's like, I've been there. Let me show you the way out.'

I want to testify to you that I know Jesus Christ is aware of your suffering. Like Moses among the Hebrews, standing with his serpent upon a staff, you merely have to have the faith to look in the right direction to find the help and hope, the compassion and the understanding you need. I want to promise you that there is indeed no place you can humanly go, with your mind, your body, or your spirit, that is out of the reach of his grace. You need but turn your eyes upward and stretch out your hand, and you will find, like Frodo drowning in the River Anduin, the humble but always-ready Samwise Gamgee's hand thrusting down to grab you and haul you, gasping and drenched, back into the boat. And he won't care that you're soaked. He will still hug you, and dry you off, and then help you cross the river.

Caught Up To The Third Heaven

'I knew a man in Christ above fourteen years ago (whether in the body, I cannot tell; or whether out of the body, I cannot tell: God knoweth;) such an one caught up to the third heaven.'

—2 Corinthians 12:2

Spend any time at all with a couple of LDS missionaries and pretty soon you're going to hear about something called the 'Kingdoms of Glory'. This is an expansion of our understanding of the afterlife, and it works like this:

Right now, after we shuffle off our mortal coil and cross to the other side of the Veil, we either go to Paradise or Outer Darkness. We have a study aid called the 'Guide to the Scriptures' that defines Paradise as 'that part of the spirit world in which the righteous spirits who have

departed from this life await the resurrection of the body' and describe it as 'a condition of happiness and peace'. Outer Darkness, by contrast, is the '... abode in the spirit world for those who were disobedient in mortality'. Which one of these we each end up in depends in large part on how close to God's presence we will be willing to stand, knowing the things we have done in our life:

> 'Therefore if that man repenteth not, and remaineth and dieth an enemy to God, the demands of divine justice do awaken his immortal soul to a lively sense of his own guilt, which doth cause him to shrink from the presence of the Lord...'
>
> —Mosiah 2:38

It's pretty easy to see this is essentially the general Christian concept of Heaven and Hell. One key difference we have in our understanding, though, is that this situation will only last until Judgement Day, at the end of the Millennial Reign. Once Judgement has been passed on each of us, we will go to our actual eternal reward, and this is where these 'Kingdoms of Glory' come in.

We have an entire section of the Doctrine &

Covenants (76, to be precise) recording a vision had by Joseph Smith and Sidney Rigdon about the kingdoms of glory. It sorts humanity into to three groups: those who were dedicated to God's principles, those who were dedicated to themselves only, and those somewhere in the middle. A lot of this breakdown can be defined in the light of the 'two greatest commandments' mentioned in Matthew 22: to love God, and love your neighbor as yourself. I'm going to start off by saying that *all we really know* about these three kingdoms is what's told us in Doctrine & Covenants Section 76 and there's only the barest of detail there. In the interest of trying to avoid putting my own spin on this (except in a few points) I'm going to try to limit myself to that.

First there is the Telestial kingdom. This is for those who loved neither God nor their neighbors and really only cared about themselves. The selfish folks that were always looking out for their own interests and damn anyone else's concerns or needs. Now this could theoretically encompass everyone from the spitefully unrepentant neighbor who borrowed your lawnmower and never gave it back to serial killers, but that's only my take on it.

The Celestial kingdom is for those dedicated to God.

For us it means people who've actually joined the Church, set their lives in a direction of supporting his work, and remained faithful, but we also know that it will be for good people who lived out their lives before they ever would have had an opportunity to hear of all this (like your great-great-great-great (etc)-grandmother in the 1700's). Folks who would have dedicated themselves if they had had the chance. Not only that, but even people living today who've passed on the opportunity, will have another chance over there to come to know the truth about God and choose to follow him. It's all in play until Judgement Day. These folks dwell in the presence of God.

We also believe that 'things sealed on earth as they are in heaven' by those with God's authority will dwell together in the Celestial kingdom, and this is why we put a lot of emphasis on sealing spouses to each other, and parents to children.

In the middle there's the Terrestrial kingdom. A place for those who were good people, but never could bring themselves to follow God, either out of pride, skepticism, or what-have-you, either now or on the other side. These people can enjoy the presence of Jesus, but not of God himself.

The Celestial kingdom has been compared to the brightness of the sun; the Terrestrial, to the moon; and the Telestial to the stars, but it's clear that's only an analogy and not some kind of literal reference. In the Gospel according to Steve I think this may allude to the notion that the denizens of the Celestial and Terrestrial kingdoms dwell together in their respective spheres (symbolized by one sun and one moon), but the Telestial guys are all kept separate since they've proven they don't know how to behave around others (symbolized by the myriad of stars).

It's another point in *my* understanding (please note this is me, and not necessarily doctrine, though as I noted before we don't have a lot of detail so I can't say it's *not* true), that these may be only some kind of 'membership' status and not an actual physical separation of these groups. Certainly elsewhere in our scriptures we know that those in the Celestial kingdom will be given charge to look after those in the other two, so there's bound to be some kind of contact there.

And another point to be made is this: Joseph Smith made it *very* clear when he wrote down this vision, that *all* of these kingdoms surpass anything we can imagine now. Even the Telestial one! So none of these are really like the

common conception of Hell.

There is a place like Hell, though, and it's called Perdition. As a matter of fact, almost the entire first half of Section 76 is devoted to describing Perdition. This *is* an eternal punishment, but you've got to work pretty hard to get there: basically, you've got to rebel fully against God, *after you've come to know him*. Perdition is for people who knew the deal, and still threw hands. People like Lucifer. Your run-of-the-mill bad guy isn't going to qualify because he would have never accepted God in the first place. He's just going to get tucked off somewhere in the Telestial kingdom where he won't bother anyone (but admittedly, for selfish folks that can be a hell all its own).

In the Church I've found there seems to be an assumption made that everyone really wants to get to the Celestial kingdom. Members get excited about it and gush about how great it's going to be to spend eternity with their families around them and carrying on God's work of managing the Universe, and seem utterly baffled when others don't share their enthusiasm. They seem to feel if folks don't want to get to the Celestial kingdom, it's only because they don't really know what it's going to be like and all we have to do is explain it more to them.

But the truth is, we *don't* know that much about it. We can surmise some things, but that's what they are— suppositions. All we know really is what is in Section 76, and a little more in Section 131. And I can tell you for a fact (especially to the members of the Church reading this): some people are *just not going to be interested.* And it isn't because they're selfish or they don't care about others.

Some people may find that Telestial kingdom attractive because they've been hurt too many times. Every interaction with another person has left me bruised and confused? People that I thought I could depend on abandoned me when I needed them the most? Why would I expose myself to that for Eternity when I can find myself a nice place (remember, even the Telestial kingdom's glory is pretty awesome) and hunker down with my dog (yes, all dogs *do* go to heaven) and forget how horrible people used to be to me? I'll be looked after, so I won't have to struggle, but neither do I have to open myself up to others' abuses again.

Or maybe they decide the Terrestrial kingdom is for them. This idea of managing the Universe is overwhelming! But I can't stand being alone... so, yeah, to live in a world much like this one, one I'm used to, but with all the selfish,

entitled idiots sequestered away? Sign me up!

The point is, *God loves his children.* All of them. And he wants to give them all they are willing to handle. And once Judgement Day has come and gone, he's not going to force anyone to take on more than they're willing, and in any case, he will take care of us, wherever we land.

A Light In Dark Places

'And now, when Moses had said these words,
Satan cried with a loud voice, and ranted
upon the earth, and commanded, saying: I
am the Only Begotten, worship me.
And it came to pass that Moses began to fear
exceedingly; and as he began to fear, he saw
the bitterness of hell....'

—Moses 1:19-20

Mother's Day 2002 was the first time I attended a service of the Church of Jesus Christ of Latter-day Saints. I was there with the guy who had been my best friend since elementary school, who had been a brother to me my entire life, Mike Eging. He had driven up from his home in Virginia to join me that day but was only able to stay for the sacrament service. As he was getting in the car for the five-hour drive home, he asked me if I wanted to stay for the Sunday School class. I told him 'I'm here to find out what this is all about, so I'm staying.' His mom

55

Jody then took me under her wing and off we went.

The lesson that day was about a guy named Balaam. It seems at the end of the Israelites' forty years of wandering they were conquering their way to the promised land when the King of Moab got alarmed and hired Balaam, a prophet, to curse Moses' mob for him. Balaam replied that he could only do what God commanded and, as he had been told not to in a vision, he declined.

The Moabite king wasn't to be outbid, though, and sent ever-more-generous offers until Balaam caved. To be fair to Balaam, he did pressure God to let him go, and was finally allowed on the condition that he only say what God told him to. Given that God became angry when he did go makes me feel that perhaps it was more of a 'go if you must, even though you know how I feel about it' kind of thing, but that's just me. Or it may have been that God could see that Balaam had a weakness for money and power and would be enticed to defy God's instructions once he got there and saw everything laid out on a table for him. (Probably the second one.)

In any case God wasn't happy about Balaam taking Moab up on their offer and set stumbling blocks in his path

to hinder him. You should read the rest of the story in Numbers 22, but this is the point I'm going to hold up on one thing: stumbling blocks.

I'm pretty sure anyone reading this has heard of how Satan tempted Eve in the Garden of Eden, so I'm not going to go into it here. It's a fairly straightforward tale of the Adversary offering great rewards for some 'small' transgression. Much the same thing happened in Jesus' fasting in the desert. But another story many, especially those not members of the Church, may never have heard, is given in Chapter 1 of the Book of Moses, in the Pearl of Great Price. Here Moses is on Mount Sanai getting the Ten Commandments and talking to God 'face to face'. God's glory is upon him so that the prophet can endure God's presence, and God went on to show Moses some of the works of his hands. 'But not all,' God explains, 'no man can behold all my works, except he behold all my glory; and no man can behold all my glory, and afterwards remain in the flesh on the earth.'

After this exposition God's presence withdrew and Moses 'fell unto the earth' and it was 'the space of many hours before Moses did again receive his natural strength like unto man'. Once he came to, he said to himself:

'But now mine own eyes have beheld God; but not my natural, but my spiritual eyes, for my natural eyes could not have beheld; for I should have withered and died in his presence; but his glory was upon me; and I beheld his face, for I was transfigured before him.'

—Moses 1:11

But then... he had a decidedly different visitation:

'And it came to pass that when Moses had said these words, behold, Satan came tempting him, saying: Moses, son of man, worship me. And it came to pass that Moses looked upon Satan and said: Who art thou?...

For behold, I could not look upon God, except his glory should come upon me, and I were transfigured before him. But I can look upon thee in the natural man....

Get thee hence, Satan, deceive me not;...

I will not cease to call upon God, I have other things to inquire of him: for his glory has been upon me, wherefore I can judge between him and thee. Depart hence, Satan.

And now, when Moses had said these words,

Satan cried with a loud voice, and ranted upon the earth, and commanded, saying: I am the Only Begotten, worship me.

And it came to pass that Moses began to fear exceedingly; and as he began to fear, he saw the bitterness of hell. Nevertheless, calling upon God, he received strength, and he commanded, saying: Depart from me, Satan... And now Satan began to tremble, and the earth shook...'

—Moses 1:12-21

It took a third time of commanding Satan to 'depart hence' before the Adversary finally left, 'wailing and gnashing his teeth'. But clearly he was all about intimidating Moses to abandon God and follow him, once he saw that he couldn't tempt him away.

Here's another story, a little closer to home: I have come to find that most people outside the Church really don't have an idea how Joseph Smith came to establish this Church. It seems a lot of folks just assume he was like most other people who do that sort of thing: some guy gets a crazy idea that he's the messiah, he convinces a handful of gullible suckers, and the thing goes viral. Or he makes the

whole thing up for fame and riches.

Well, not so much: in 1820 Joseph was a young boy of fourteen scraping out an existence on a small farm in upstate New York. There were a lot of revivals going on then and sects of Protestantism would set up tents next to each other in a field, county-fair style, and preach their contending interpretations of scripture to all who would listen as the crowds milled from one tent to another. It was like speed dating, but for church.

It was these sometimes vehement differences of opinion of the various Christian denominations that caused the young, confused Joseph to pick up the Bible and read for himself—a rather smart thing to do when you think about it, and I find it very significant that he got all the way to the general epistle of James, which is almost near the end, before he found his answer: go and pray about it (James 1:5). So, not long after, he went to a quiet place in the woods behind his home and did just that. And this is what happened:

> 'After I had retired to the place where I had previously designed to go, having looked around me, and finding myself alone, I

kneeled down and began to offer my heart to God. I had scarcely done so, when immediately I was seized upon by some power which entirely overcame me, and had such an astonishing influence over me as to bind my tongue so I could not speak. Thick darkness gathered around me, and it seemed for a time as if I were doomed to a sudden destruction.

But, exerting all my powers to call upon God to deliver me out of the power of this enemy which had seized upon me, and at the very moment when I was ready to sink into despair and abandon myself to destruction—not to an imaginary ruin, but to the power of some actual being from the unseen world, who had such marvelous power as I had never before felt in any being—just at that moment of great alarm, I saw a pillar of light exactly over my head, above the rightness of the sun, which descended gradually until it fell upon me.

It no sooner appeared than I found myself delivered from the enemy which held me bound.'

—Joseph Smith History 1:15-17

Joseph goes on to say that within that pillar of light he saw two figures, much as had Stephen nearly two millennia before. There's a *lot* more to the rest of this story (especially about all the ridicule, harassment, and antagonism in his community, and eventually the world at large [look up Missouri's Extermination Order]) but again, I'm going to stop here to focus on one thing: opposition.

Knowing these stories caused me a fair bit of confusion when I was first investigating the Church. If God was wont to put stumbling blocks in your path to keep you from doing something stupid, and Satan was willing to shake the earth and swamp you with darkness to keep you from doing something good, *how do you know which one is responsible for the roadblock you're facing in the moment?*

The answer lies in knowing about the Plan of Salvation (which relates to those kingdoms of glory). The Book of Revelations mentions a 'war fought in heaven'; we understand this to refer to a battle (of some kind, I don't know if it was with words, fists, or bolts of lightning) fought amongst God's children after the Grand Council I mentioned on page 43 (yes, I will be getting to that). We had all heard the plan, and many of us thought it was a

workable idea and lined up. However, 'a third of God's children' felt Lucifer had a better idea with just dragging us all along the way and rebelled with him. Apparently they felt so strongly that *everyone* should be brought back to God's presence whether we liked it or not that they were willing to ignore everyone else's feelings on the matter. Because they knew better what was best for us, I suppose.

The essential line in the sand was this: God wanted us to *have a choice.* He would love for us to all follow his teachings, but he wanted us to do so because we saw the value in them and chose to, on our own. To God our most precious quality was our 'agency', our privilege to be agents unto ourselves and make our own decisions.

Lucifer wanted to *force* us to toe the line. He didn't give two shekels for our opinions, our wants, or whether or not we might prefer *not* to be in the Celestial kingdom when it was all said and done.

And that's the key: God may want to encourage you to stay on the path, he may *really, really* want to encourage you to stay on the path (go back and read Balaam's story, or Paul's conversion in Acts Chapter 9, or Alma's in Alma Chapter 36), but he's still got to leave you a way around

that stumbling block if you really want to go on. A war was fought for your right to choose for yourself.

But the Adversary doesn't care about *your* choice, only what *he* wants for you, and he'll do whatever it takes to either lead you away with temptations or force you off with fear.

So: if you're trying your best and the way forward looks difficult, it's probably too good to be true. If it looks impossible, *that* is the right path. Stick with it.

PART TWO

"It is a radio... for speaking to God!"

—René Belloq,
Raiders of the Lost Ark

Seeing Is Believing...
Isn't It?

'But if he will not hear thee, then take with thee
one or two more, that in the mouth of two or
three witnesses every word may be established.'
—Matthew 18:16

Seeing is believing! Such is the old saying. "Show me the money!" Another expression, popular some years ago, that also asks for something real and tangible in place of hot air. "The proof is in the pudding!" An older one, but nevertheless asking for the same thing: Proof! We live in a society that is infatuated with *proof*, with the notion that things *can* be proven, that they *should* be proven. That if something isn't in my hand it isn't real.

Once many years ago I took a course in negotiating skills. The instructor was a champion businessman, and very accustomed to negotiating for his company. He told a

story about once, when he was out playing golf, a small boy came up to him selling golf balls. This gentleman decided to practice his skills by negotiating his best price—that is, until the young man opened his box of golf balls and displayed the prices clearly marked on the inside of the lid. The instructor pointed out to us that it's hard to negotiate with something written in black and white. We *like* things that are written down. They're tangible. They're 'hard evidence'.

As a society we love it so much that this country is awash in lawyers who make their living by demonstrating the truth of things by *proving* them with evidence. And don't forget that some of the most popular TV shows are crime dramas where the bad guy is caught by the heroes' relentless search for *proof*. And these can all trace their ancestry back to one of the most popular fictional characters of all time: Sherlock Holmes, who was the epitome of impassionate, objective, logical reasoning. And it's not just in judicial matters that we like *proof*.

Over the last few hundred years science has made great strides in many different fields, and our lives have changed largely for the better. And if you look at how science works, it's no real mystery—it's by *proof*. Proof is at

the heart of the scientific method: that only those things that *can* be proven should be accepted. But for our world that's not enough. Never mind a thing is proven, it has to be *verified*: proven over and over. Billions of dollars are spent every year to verify, re-verify, and re-re-verify the findings of researchers. Thousands of academics make their livings this way. For the record I have a great deal of respect for the scientific method. As a doctor I depend on evidence-based medicine, and before that I earned my undergrad degree in mathematics, the most rigorous scientific discipline of them all.

This obsession with *proof* was never more clearly illustrated to me than the time some years ago when I saw a TV commercial going on about the health benefits of vitamin C. Now I thought everyone knew about vitamin C. But the announcer made his point by stacking up over a hundred research reports *proving* that vitamin C was good for you. All well and good, but I thought, 'Who thought a hundred studies were necessary?? And who authorized paying for them all?' Are we really a people that need a hundred different research studies to prove vitamin C is good for us? Wouldn't four or five do the trick?

Or three?

For many years we have been taught that science is so powerful because it can prove things are real. We don't need to rely on guesswork and supposition any longer. Now don't get me wrong! In many cases this is true, and the scientific method has made our collective standard of living much better. For one thing, it makes it possible for me to sit at home and watch movies on TV about Sherlock Holmes!

But there is a time and place where everything belongs. This means conversely there is a time and place where things don't, and in some ways the attitude that things must be proven can be a hindrance. If I had a nickel for every time I heard someone say, 'If God is real why doesn't he show himself and *prove* it?' I would never have had to go to medical school. It's a common enough challenge from those who do not believe. But it seems like a valid question—why doesn't he? If everyone loves proof so well and he wants us to believe in him, showing himself would shut a lot of people up, wouldn't it? But to answer that question we need to answer a much more fundamental query. One I had long before I was even investigating the LDS Church. One that many very wise people have thought about, examined, dissected and put back together, and still not come up with a satisfactory answer:

Why are we here?

Despite all the trouble people have had with this it's surprisingly not a hard question to answer. Once you know you wonder how you never saw it. I'll go into this in more detail in the last chapter, but for now I'll just say that I never really understood the *question* until I quit looking at it from our common cultural view of God ruling over us like some feudal lord, and started considering it as a parent raising his children.

As parents we have a desire that our children will grow up to lead happy, successful lives, however we may define happiness and success. We know from our own experience that there are certain rules they must learn. Rules like 'Share'. 'Don't hit your sister'. 'Clean up your own mess'. Basic kindergarten stuff that takes a minute to learn and a lifetime to master. The kind of stuff we call a 'moral code'. And as parents it's our job to instill these rules into our children.

So how do we know when the kids have *got it?* That they have seen the value of these rules and taken them to heart, and are not just behaving because we're in the room watching them? It's simple—when we see them use these

rules when *they don't think we're watching*. When we hear about how they went the extra mile at school or at work without being asked. When their friend's mom calls from the sleepover to report how *nice* they were. That's when we can breathe a sigh of relief and feel we've done our job.

But what about God? He wants to make sure we all know how to conduct ourselves so that existence in Heaven can be all it's cracked up to be. No one wants to spend eternity living by that guy that always borrows your stuff and never brings it back, right? So... what do you do if you're an all-powerful deity that sees and knows everything, and your children know that you see and know everything? How can you arrange for them to act on their own without them feeling like you're looking over their shoulders all the time (even if you can)?

Like this: you make them a world away from everything else and put them there with no memory of where they came from. Where the only thing they know about your rules and goals is from the secondhand testimonies of a chosen few. That way they won't know for sure if you're real or not, and if they want to badly enough, they'll be able to convince themselves you aren't.

This is why we will never get *proof*—the hard physical evidence that people like to ask for—that God exists. Because then everyone would *know* He's watching and walk the line very carefully. No one would ever show their true colors. I recently saw a comment on the internet that, if everyone were wearing body cams, no one would behave the way they do. It's very true, and even has a name: The Hawthorne Effect (there's actually an interesting story on how that was named and I encourage you to look it up). It would take away our choice to act as we wish because we would all feel compelled to behave simply by God's constant presence. That would defeat the entire purpose of creating this world in the first place.

It is also exactly the thing the Adversary proposed. For those of you not members of the Church, I'll clarify: in the Pearl of Great Price, the Book of Abraham, we learn there was a 'Grand Council' held before the creation of the world. I mentioned it before, but here's a little more detail: We were all there, to hear for the first time the proposal of the creation of this world and how and why it was going to test us.

A savior was called for. Lucifer stepped up and stated he would run us all through the program and make sure

not a single one of us fell by the wayside, that we all would pass the test and return to God's presence. Sounds nice, but the problem was that he was basically going to give us the answers to the test. One might argue a more accurate analogy was that he was going to grab our hands to write the 'correct' answers whether we wanted to or not.

Then Jesus stepped up and said he would show the way, rather than herd us along it, even though some of us wouldn't make it all the way back. God chose Jesus because the whole purpose of the plan was to teach us the value of looking out for each other and no one learns anything when the answers are just handed to them. Lucifer got angry, rebelled, and a war in heaven ensued. You can see that having us actually *learn*, rather than just go through the motions, was much more important to God.

Yet God does show himself to prophets. So what's the deal? What is so special about prophets? Why do they get to see God face to face if doing so makes the whole test pointless?

Because it's not fair testing us if we don't know what the questions are! So *someone* has to know what's on the test.

Then how are they picked? Are they perfect? Of course not—none of us is perfect. Moses killed a man in anger and then fled the legal justice of Egypt. Paul actively tried to destroy the early church. There are several places in the Doctrine & Covenants where Joseph Smith admits he was warned by God he needed to straighten up and fly right. So what sets prophets apart?

Faith.

That's what we are being tested on, but if you already have 'enough', whatever that is, then you get to see God because you have already proven yourself. The Book of Mormon tells of the appearance of Jesus to someone identified only as 'the brother of Jared':

> '... sufficeth me to say that Jesus showed
> himself unto this man in the spirit, even after
> the manner and in the likeness of the same
> body even as he showed himself unto the
> Nephites...
> And because of the knowledge of this man he
> could not be kept from beholding within the
> veil; and he saw the finger of Jesus, which,
> when he saw, he fell with fear; for he knew that

it was the finger of the Lord; and he had faith no longer, for he knew, nothing doubting. Wherefore, having this perfect knowledge of God, he could not be kept from within the veil; therefore he saw Jesus; and he did minister unto him.

—Ether 3:17-20

This man had something called 'perfect knowledge'. Since it was 'perfect' it was not of this world, so it was an 'eternal' knowledge. It came from his own testimony, a faith so strong that the proof was not in his hands, but in his heart. Ordinary knowledge, the sort of knowledge our society values, is 'believing because proof exists'. Faith is believing *without* proof, the 'hope of things not seen'. Now it says in this passage that 'he had faith no longer, for he knew, nothing doubting'. What does *this* mean?

It means if you have *proof* of the Lord, you have knowledge, but then you can no longer have *faith*, which is a hope in things not *proven*. Regaining the ability to show your faith would require the *proof* be taken away. Even the memory of it! So, gaining physical *proof* of the Lord's existence is a kind of 'point of no return' in our spiritual progression, and once we get *proof* we will never be able to

show if we could have had *faith*. It's like ending the test before we can answer the question. How can anyone ever know then if we would have got the right answer?

The proof will come, someday. But that day will be the Second Coming. Meanwhile we are supposed to have faith. How we manage on that issue I'm pretty sure will be one of the questions we will be asked on the other side of the Veil. Asking for proof of the Lord's existence is really shortchanging yourself. But it's not an easy thing to do, to believe without proof, to take things on faith. Even the best of us can find it difficult. When Jesus returned to his disciples after the Resurrection Thomas had to be shown *proof*, and caught a little flak for it:

> But Thomas, one of the twelve, called Didymus, was not with them when Jesus came.
> The other disciples therefore said unto him, We have seen the Lord. But he said unto them, Except I shall see in his hands the print of the nails, and put my finger into the print of the nails, and thrust my hand into his side, I will not believe.
> And after eight days again his disciples were

within, and Thomas with them: [then] came
Jesus, the doors being shut, and stood in the
midst, and said, Peace [be] unto you.
Then saith he to Thomas, Reach hither thy
finger, and behold my hands; and reach hither
thy hand, and thrust [it] into my side: and be
not faithless, but believing.
And Thomas answered and said unto him,
My Lord and my God.
Jesus saith unto him, Thomas, because thou
hast seen me, thou hast believed: blessed [are]
they that have not seen, and [yet] have
believed.

—John 20:24-29

It's pretty clear that we are expected to *believe first* and
see later. The same way the brother of Jared saw because he
already had 'perfect knowledge', not ordinary knowledge.

In the corporate world it has become fashionable to
go on retreats where the employees get involved in trust-
building exercises, like standing in the middle of a group,
closing your eyes and falling backwards for them to catch
you. It's their way of teaching you to have faith in your
fellow workers. But the key is you have to close your eyes

78

first! Withholding *proof* is the only way to make our faith stronger. Then, by demonstrating that faith, we can show that we have learned the lessons we have come here to learn, and when we're done here, we can go on to all the blessings that are waiting for us on the other side.

Range Day
At
Fort Knox

*'And while I was thus struggling in the spirit,
behold, the voice of the Lord came to my mind
again, saying: I will visit thy brethren according to their diligence in keeping my commandments....'*

—Enos 1:10

Living a religious life is *hard*. On a daily basis. Hard
enough that a question we as members of the LDS
Church are asked (and often ask ourselves, truth be told),
is 'why must I try *so* hard, *all the time*? Why must I be
always so careful? Why is it even necessary to 'endure to the
end'?'

It seems to me that there are mainly two reasons for

this feeling. On the one hand, we may feel overwhelmed: 'I know I will never be perfect, I've been told this time and again, why do I try so hard for something that is unattainable here on earth?' On the other hand, we may simply feel lazy: 'Why should I put in the effort? J.C.'s just gonna pick up the slack for me anyway?' I'm going to try to answer both of those questions with one story. But first, a little context, so you know what kind of a sandbox we're playing in.

There's been some debate in religious circles about whether or not inanimate matter has the capacity to willfully respond to the word of God, but certainly he established the rules of the universe: the constants of gravitation, the strong and weak nuclear forces, and the twenty-three other physical properties that rule the motion of subatomic particles and supergalactic clusters alike, so I presume he knows how to use them to his advantage. In any case, God speaks, and Matter obeys.

On the other hand, it's pretty safe to say that every single *living* thing in the wide vastness of the universe bears some small degree of what we could legitimately call intelligence. We know this from scripture, though the references are scattered throughout the LDS' standard

works, and it would take me more than the space I have available to review them (and the point would only be a tangent anyway). Suffice it to say that Abraham explained that a living spirit is an organized intelligence, and Moses revealed that all living things were created in spirit before they were placed on the earth. Thus it is that each spark of life is able to interact willfully with God and, at least in theory, has the capacity to defy God, should it so choose. Not that they do. Only humanity has the propensity to, as it says in 2 Nephi 10:3, 'crucify their God.' Everyone else seems perfectly happy with things. Why is that?

I would suggest that this is because God's word is inviolate. Once he has spoken, his word stands. If he were to go back on it, as it says in 3 Nephi 28:38, 'he would cease to be God.' He is 'the same yesterday, today and forever.' He is impeccably reliable. This is why he has the trust, faith and support of every single living entity in the universe capable of acting for itself, and why they are eager to carry out his will. With the exception of us, that is.

Now I think it's worth taking a moment to digress, to make a distinction that being careful in your relationship with this Being, this Spirit Father, does not require you to be fearful. He actually wants you to succeed, as it says in the

Old Testament:

> '... prove me now herewith, saith the Lord of
> hosts, if I will not open you the windows of
> heaven, and pour you out a blessing that there
> shall not be room enough to receive it'.
>
> —Malachi 3:10

But what he wants to give you is 'all that he has' (John 16:15 and Doctrine & Covenants 84:38). That carries with it a great responsibility, and you have to be ready for it, physically and mentally, and he cannot compromise on your training.

And now I want to tell you the story of Private Forrest and Private Wadsworth (naturally not their real names). But again, a little context, so you know what kind of sandbox we're playing in:

Cavalry scout training in the US Army in the late 1990's consisted of a 16-week course at the US Armor Training Center in Ft. Knox, Kentucky. It included all of Army Basic Training as well as those tasks specific to forward battlefield reconnaissance. It was a demanding course, both physically and mentally. We had to learn

twenty-four separate and distinct weapons systems; map reading and land navigation; operation of radio equipment and conducting encoded communications; setting up defenses for forward observation posts that were often expected to be miles ahead of the main battle line; assessments of roads and bridges for the units coming up behind us and weaknesses in hostile emplacements ahead of us; tactical movement; patrolling; first aid; basic demolitions; and our primary mission, calling for and directing artillery fire. There were one hundred and forty-one recruits embarking on this journey in Charlie Troop, Fifth Squadron, Fifteenth Cavalry in the fall of 1997. I was in the third of four platoons, and one of my squadmates was a young kid from Brooklyn, New York, named Private Forrest.

Now Private Forrest had experienced a lot of challenges growing up in the inner city. And to be perfectly honest, and by no means judgmental, he was not the sharpest knife in the drawer. But he tried. He put everything he had, however much that may have been, into everything he did. I'm pretty sure he felt if he was not going to make it in the Army, he probably was not going to make it anywhere.

By contrast we also had, in another platoon in our troop, Private Wadsworth, a midwestern suburban kid from what most would call a 'good background'. He clearly didn't want to be there and was noticeably less motivated.

About a month into training, we reached the point of qualifying with our rifles. This was a fundamental skill required of everyone from the newest recruit to the most seasoned general. We started off with some days of mastering the care and operation of the M16A1: how to break it down, clean it, reassemble it (in under three minutes), perform a function check, acquire a sight picture, trigger squeeze, effective ranges, rates of fire, and so forth. This training culminated in Range Day. On Range Day you would be taken to the firing range and handed two magazines of twenty rounds each. In your lane, over the span of a scant few minutes, you would be presented with forty pop-up targets. Forty rounds, forty targets. You had to hit twenty-three of them in order to pass, and you would have three opportunities to make this happen. If you failed you would be transferred to another troop that had started after yours in the curriculum, and some weeks later when they had their Range Day you would have another opportunity to make your three attempts, and if you failed that, you went home, and that would be that. No veteran

status. No GI Bill. Nothing.

Range Day for Charlie Troop came the day after Thanksgiving. It was cold, about twenty degrees, and there was a stiff wind blowing (because there is *always* a stiff wind blowing on Range Day). We were out in the wide-open field of the firing range with only a three-sided corrugated tin shelter over some bleachers to protect us from the elements.

It took most of the day to run all of us through the range the first time, and then to give the ones that didn't make it their second attempt. By late afternoon First, Second, and Fourth Platoons had managed to run all their recruits through, pass or fail, and were headed back to the barracks for a warm dinner and a little down time. Not so Third Platoon. We were in the bleachers, waiting for Private Forrest to make his third attempt.

Which he failed.

But then the drill sergeants did something unexpected. They came to us, as a platoon, and asked us if we wanted them to give Private Forrest one more chance.

For the record I seriously doubt Private Forrest had

asked them to do this. That wasn't the kind of guy he was. Even if he had, knowing my drill sergeants (especially Drill Sergeant Smith) they would have flatly said 'no'. But Sgt. Smith was just the kind of rough-on-the-outside-thoughtful-on-the-inside kind of guy that would have decided himself to ask us if we would be willing to sustain this young kid from Brooklyn. Even though they knew damn well that if we did this time, we might very well have to another time. We knew it, too. We would be the ones to carry his burden tomorrow if we gave him a break today.

By now it was after 6pm. It was dark. We were cold. And this was against protocol.

But we trusted our drill sergeants' judgment, and we knew they would keep their word. They were impeccably reliable. If they gave Private Forrest the chance, and he passed, as far as they cared it would be as if he had made it on the first try.

Over the preceding weeks we had learned something about teamwork, unit cohesiveness, and 'helping your buddy'. And we had seen how hard Private Forrest tried with everything he did, and how self-aware he was of his limitations. We knew the respect he had for what we were

all trying to accomplish by his sheer humble determination to keep going. And so it was that, to a man, Third Platoon stood up and said 'yes'.

So, they ran him through again. And he failed.

And we ran him through *again*. And again. And again! I think it was on about the seventh, or maybe the eighth, attempt that Private Forrest finally got his twenty-three targets and passed his rifle qualification. Certainly, it was after 10 o'clock that night by the time we left the range. Third Platoon was starving, we were chilled to the bone, but we were not miserable: our Private Forrest was still in the ranks.

You can see that Charlie Troop's drill sergeants didn't lower the standard to suit a struggling recruit. Nor did they compromise on Private Forrest's training. They knew the responsibility they were about to give this kid from Brooklyn was great. After all, an artillery barrage is a fearful thing. They just kept at him, for as long as Private Forrest was willing to try, and as long as we were willing to sustain, until he was able to attain the standard. They kept working with him, just as cold and hungry as we were, and I might add, patiently (I don't think I heard any of the three raise

their voice once that night) until he finally got it right.

Private Wadsworth, the midwestern kid, though, had put up a consistently lackluster and excuse-laden effort over the preceding weeks. He failed his three attempts that day, was transferred to another troop, failed there as well, and eventually went home.

I mentioned earlier that Cav Scout training was demanding. You should know that of the one hundred and forty-one recruits that started the course in Charlie Troop, only ninety-six finished it. We lost one-third of our complement, forty-five in all, who, like Private Wadsworth, wouldn't keep up, and washed out along the way.

But Private Forrest was not one of them. On the twenty-eighth day of February, 1998, Charlie Troop graduated, and Private Forrest marched out on the parade ground with the rest of Third Platoon, received his certificate from the hands of his drill sergeants, and walked away a Cavalryman.

The lesson I want to leave you with is this: In my years in the Church, I have seen a lot of similarity between the way things are done here, and how we did them in the Army, at least attitude-wise. If you try to excuse yourself

like Private Wadsworth, you'll be left to your own devices. As it says in Helaman 4:13: 'and because of this their great wickedness, and their boastings in their own strength, they were left in their own strength; therefore they did not prosper, but were afflicted and smitten, and driven before the Lamanites, until they had lost possession of almost all their lands.'

But if you are willing to stay humble and put in the effort, as much as you can, no matter how impossible, or even *trivial,* the task may seem, there will be helping hands lining up for you. To help you be brave, to do the hard things, and sometimes to intercede on your behalf with the powers-that-be when it's just too much. It may only be a few people around you or maybe it's every single living thing in the vast universe, but they are there, your own Third Platoon, who have taken you in as family because you are a child of the Creator they revere, and you have shown that you respect him as much as they do. For that reason, they are actually genuinely eager to see you succeed and will sustain you as you try, and try, and try again, whether it be your third attempt, your seventh attempt, or your seventy-times-seventh attempt.

Profiting By Prophet-ing

'Before I formed thee in the belly I knew thee;
and before thou camest forth out of the womb I
sanctified thee, and I ordained thee a prophet
unto the nations.'

—Jeremiah 1:5

In my time in the Church I've found it's always something else to hear words straight from a prophet. I've found the counsel I have received has been very enlightening and timely, and it pains me that most people I know who LDS are not, or even just folks in our general culture, don't even really know what a prophet is. For most of them the word brings to mind an image of a Gandalf, or a Nostradamus: a wizened old coot with ragged robes and crazy eyes that spouts cryptic rhymes that—we hope—will somehow magically make sense to us when we reach the critical turning point in our journey.

But that is definitely *not* what a prophet is. He's not a fortune-teller. If he's supposed to tell us what's coming, hiding it in an obscurely-worded limerick makes for an entertaining story, but it's a good way to set up your hero for failure.

The LDS Church defines a prophet rather poetically (but maybe a little obtusely) as not a *fore-teller*, but a *forth-teller*, one who brings forth the word of God. I think it's a little clearer to compare the words of a prophet to those of a wiser sibling/friend/colleague who tells you with absolute certainty that the stupid thing you are about to do is bound to land you in hot water.

In an earlier chapter I talked about our purpose here, that this life is an education. As part of that we are presented with lessons, and then we are tested on those lessons. The prophet then is much like a teacher in class. He's not going to just hand us the answers, nor is he going to tell us when the test is so we can cut class that day. But he is going to make sure we have the knowledge and skills we need to *pass* the test.

I've spent an awful lot of time in school, and I've seen this scenario play out hundreds of times: The teacher

writes something on the board. He underlines it, circles it, reads it aloud, and then turns to you with a wink and a raised eyebrow and says, '*You* should write that down, it *might be on the test.*' Of course he knows it will be on the test. But he's ensuring that *you* know it will be.

In October 2018 Russell M. Nelson, current president of the Church, said, 'Wait till next year, and then the next year. Eat your vitamin pills. Get some rest.' How relevant is that, looking back on the pandemic of 2020? He didn't tell us what was coming. For all I know he may not himself have known *exactly* what was coming. But he knew what we needed to do to prepare for it.

Several times in scripture I've read the passage, 'he who hath an ear, let him hear.' This is almost always uttered in connection with prophecies of the latter days, or sometimes in a condemnation of those who reject the prophetic warnings of the latter days, as in 'they do not have ears to hear.' Matthew 13: 36-43 is a perfect example. We have been warned. Actually, we have been 'being warned' for a long time now. What we do with that warning is up to us. It always has been, but I encourage everyone to take the hint seriously.

Most of us in the Church have heard stories along the lines of a guy driving down the road who was impressed to stop and get a gallon of milk and then drop it off at a random house, and how the people there had a hungry child with no way to feed it and regarded the man as an angel for answering their prayers. Or the one told by Sister Jean A. Stevens of the Primary General Presidency where she related how she had been driving down a dark road, saw a young boy walking along it, and was inspired to stop and ask if he needed help. He did, and had been praying hard for it.

Now don't get me wrong. These anecdotes are enlightening, uplifting and illustrative, but they are also rather dramatic. Most of us won't have stories like that to tell, and actually that is the rule. God prefers to work by subtle means whenever he can. In Alma 37:6 it says: 'by small and simple things are great things brought to pass'. Do you think there's a particular reason for this approach? I do.

If there were big flashy miracles happening all day long, it wouldn't take long for belief in God to no longer be a matter of faith. It would be easy to trust in His sustaining might because we would see it happening all

around us without even trying. Where would be the test of our faith then? When could we prove ourselves that we can have faith, if we were never called upon to exercise it? But having to act in faith can be scary. Stepping out into the unknown, as it were.

Take my word for it, it's easier if you are in regular communication with God. One of the most consistent, and persistent, messages we in the Church hear is to maintain that channel of communication: to send prayers up, and pay attention when the impressions come back down. That second half is not an easy thing, and I know it! As Paul said in 1 Corinthians, 'we see through a glass, darkly'. Granted there's a good reason for that (go back two chapters for a refresher) but it doesn't make it any less frustrating. Or scary.

But that's one of our challenges in this life: having faith to listen to the Spirit, no matter what it tells you. Sometimes it tells you to get up off your couch and go do something material to help someone.

But sometimes, many times, it tells you instead...

'Peace, be still, and know that I am God.'

Now you may be inclined to ask, 'why do I need to work so hard to listen to the Spirit?' It's simple, really. Another of our basic understandings in the Church is that we are *all* prophets, to some degree, *within our own sphere of responsibility.* The president of the LDS Church is responsible for the whole kit and kaboodle, so he gets revelations for the Church as a whole. The ward bishop gets revelations for the ward he leads, and you are entitled to get revelations regarding yourself and your household. That's one aspect of this 'gift of the Holy Ghost' I mentioned a while back. So, you want to learn to listen. This life is a test, and quite often it is a test of our courage. Our resolve. We may not be called upon to face an angry Pharoah, but we may be impressed to pay our tithing when there's not enough money in the bank to pay the rent. Or speak out when we want to shrink into the shadows.

But testing people's courage means putting them in a position that makes them afraid. There is no other way to muster one's courage. But when people allow their fears to take over, they can do rash things. And that can be bad.

On 28 June 1914 Archduke Ferdinand of Austria was assassinated by a Serbian. Because so many of the Great Powers of Europe—Great Britain, France, Germany,

Russia, and Austria—had strategic interests in the region, they all had treaties with the many smaller countries there, so when Austria declared war on Serbia for the assassination, all these major players were suddenly called upon to fulfill their treaty obligations. When one small country was threatened by a Great Power, another Great Power was already pledged to come to their aid. Within a matter of weeks these big countries were stationing troops on each others' borders, like dads squaring off over a quarrel of their children.

The armies were massive. Hundreds of thousands each, with new mechanized equipment. In order to get them to their staging areas before their enemies could get to theirs, they used the fastest mass transit they had: the railroads. But that required intricate and precise coordination of timetables to make sure everything got to the front at the same time, so men weren't standing around without ammo... or food, or shelter. But these timetables would allow for no disruptions.

Near the end of July Kaiser Wilhelm was having second thoughts. He asked his Chief of the General Staff von Moltke if they were doing the right thing. If it was too late to stop? von Moltke reportedly got pale in the face and

responded in a tizzy that it was indeed too late to turn back—if they stopped now the timetables would be thrown into chaos that would take weeks to sort out. The army would be scattered and disorganized and unable to fight... and the French and British would get the drop on them. And so out of fear the Germans went ahead with their mobilization and on 28 July they crossed into Belgium.

By the end of the war well over 30 million people were dead or injured, directly or indirectly, and a continent had been bankrupted of its youth. And as if that wasn't bad enough, the privations of that war led to the rise of the Nazis, and World War II, which was even worse.

Or maybe the problem is just not listening at all and going forward in overconfidence in yourself:

In the Book of Mormon, Mormon Chapter 4, we have the tale of how the Nephites of a city named (oddly enough) Desolation launched a pre-emptive attack against their perennial enemies, the Lamanites. The Lamanites were able to stand against the Nephites and in fact drove them back, and right out of Desolation. The Nephites regrouped at a city named Teancum and, when the

Lamanites followed them there the following year, were able to repulse them. This victory (after their initial unprovoked aggression, mind you) made the Nephites rather boastful in their military prowess. They plucked up the courage to retake Desolation and thought very highly of themselves when they won. But two years later the Lamanites returned with a bigger army. They took Desolation *and* Teancum, and sacrificed the women and children to idols. The Nephites pulled themselves together and drove them out one more time, and for about eight years there was peace.

But from there things were pretty much downhill: The war flared up again and the Nephites were driven 'like dew before the sun'. They were able to hold in fallback positions here and there in their flight, but everything they left behind was destroyed. After five more years of combat the Nephites were routed and those who couldn't keep up with the retreat were simply cut down.

Over the next four years their general Mormon gathered the dregs of their people (men, women and children) at a hill called Cumorah, and there they made their last stand. By the time that battle was over only fifteen Nephites survived. These few were eventually hunted

down like dogs and the Nephites as a people were extinct.

How many lives were lost at Cumorah? By Mormon's count, 230,000 warriors alone. *Just in that battle.* Not counting the women and children, and not counting all the suffering during the trouble over the preceding two decades.

So that's what happens when people let their fear—or their bravado—get the better of them. The solution is to not let yourself be guided by your impulses, but to...

> '... study it out in your mind, then you must ask me if it be right, and if it is right I will cause that your bosom shall burn within you; therefore, you shall feel that it is right.'
>
> —Doctrine & Covenants 9:8

There's a side note I want to emphasize here: we are encouraged to 'study it out in our minds', to *come up with a solution ourselves, to the best of our ability.* And then ask if our solution is good. Then we take that answer and either run with it, or go back and think on it more.

There's an anonymous poem that applies here in a general sense:

With thoughtless and impatient hands
We tangle up the plans
The Lord hath wrought.
And when we cry in pain He saith,
'Be quiet, man, while I untie the knot.'"

My Check-Engine Light Is On

'Be not weary in well-doing: for in due season we shall reap, if we faint not.'

—Galatians 6:9

Early LDS Leader pop quiz! Tell me everything you know about Joseph Coe, Peter Haws, and Amasa Lyman. And... go!

Nothing? All these gents are mentioned in the Doctrine & Covenants. Does that ring any bells? (To those of you not members of the Church, don't feel left out. I doubt anyone but a dyed-in-the-wool scriptorian would remember these guys.)

Alright, then, let's see what we know about them. We'll start with Joseph Coe: he was a member of the first standing council of the Church; in 1831 he served short missions to New York and Missouri; and in August 1831

he assisted in laying the cornerstones for the temple in Independence, Missouri. In 1834 he was called to the presiding high council in Kirtland. In 1835 he provided $800 of the $2400 used by the Church to purchase the papyri which contained the Book of Abraham, now a part of the Pearl of Great Price.

But after the collapse of the Kirtland Safety Society in a financial depression he dissented from the Church and apparently caused enough trouble to be formally excommunicated in December 1838. I don't know what he did, specifically, but you don't get excommunicated just because you don't show up on Sunday. Either you request in writing to be removed, or you actively fight against the Church and *are* removed.

Peter Haws was involved in actually building the temple in Nauvoo, Illinois, but left the Church in 1849 and eventually moved to California where he died in 1862.

Amasa Lyman spent some time as one of the counselors in the leadership of the High Priest Quorum. He was a member of Zion's Camp, a missionary, was ordained an apostle on August 20, 1842, and was a Counselor for Joseph Smith from February 1843 until

Smith's death in 1844. Then in 1867 he began preaching sermons basically denying the reality and the necessity of the Atonement. He had been previously disciplined for this behavior and, as he was going against his previous word to stop, he was stripped of his apostleship. He then started associating himself with another faith and as a result was excommunicated in 1870.

So, what do these men have in common? At one point they were all faithful, motivated members of the Church—enough to be ordained elders and called as missionaries, high council members and even as apostles—and yet at some point for various reasons they fell away. Men who were good enough to warrant mention in canonical scripture but have since been forgotten. Whose heat of their passion for the work sputtered out like the ignition coil of a '97 Yugo.

There are all sorts of reasons why this can happen. There's a parable told in both the Gospel of Mark and the Gospel of Matthew about sowing seeds: some seeds landed by the wayside and were immediately scrounged by the birds. Some fell on good ground, put down their roots and up their leaves, and grew strong. And then there were some that landed in stony ground and sprouted almost

immediately, but the roots weren't deep enough and they withered when the weather turned bad. Finally, there were some that landed among thorns and were choked out by weeds.

That's not a big deal if you're talking about keeping up with your weekly book club meeting. Maybe you joined and then found they are all into reading Stephen R. Donaldson when you were hoping more for Terry Pratchett. Or a golf club, and you found everyone was a pretentious jerk. Or whatever... I'm sure we all have a group we got into and then found a reason to quit. Maybe several.

But the Church is different. I know I'm in it because I firmly believe this is the one true church on earth with God's own authority. And the work is too important: it is the salvation of the entire human race. It is nothing less than the redemption and rescue of every last man, woman and child that *ever* lived. One of the reasons our missionary efforts center around discussions of core elements of our doctrine, and encourage one to explore their own feelings about them, is so that a potential convert knows what they are getting into. So that if you *don't* feel it's for you, you don't go through that trouble in the first place.

I might add a piece of guidance for anyone investigating the Church (especially if you're in the process right now of talking to missionaries): we firmly hold to the notion that God will force no one to Heaven. We aren't a 'join or perish' kind of operation. So if you're looking at all this and it doesn't fit, it's okay to tell your missionaries that it isn't for you. Just keep in mind that the Church is made up of people, and people have their faults and foibles. These missionaries are kids, basically, in that 18-to-24-year-old insurance bracket. They're excited to bring you the good news and at times their inexperienced enthusiasm can be a bit much. They may not comprehend why you're not jazzed as well and may have difficulty taking 'no' for an answer. Don't hold it against them, just cut them a break and clearly explain your reasons.

But moving on: When I was a mission leader, I made a point of explaining to my crew that finding converts may have been their stated *task*, but it wasn't their actual *purpose*. Many of these kids grew up in LDS families and had no real idea how other people lived. They had no concept of the struggles other folks had faced (and conquered).

I made sure they knew they were actually in the field to meet with people not of the Church and to *learn these*

things (among other stuff, like how the Church functions on a daily basis [meetings... lots of them, but that's not relevant here]). If folks didn't have the passion for the work, give them a break... and circle back in a couple years to see how they're doing. And wash, rinse, repeat.

I pointed out to them that if they were to return home after two years without a single baptism on record, but they gained an appreciation for the depth and breadth of human experience, their mission was a success. After all, you can't show someone the way to a better world if you don't know where they're starting from.

To those of us who are in and are feeling that lurching sputter, we need to regain that passion we had when we joined. Whether we felt the pressure of a half dozen generations of pioneers, or *we* were the pioneer in our own family, we joined for a reason. We made a decision to give it a chance, and *then* we were interviewed to make sure our reasons were legitimate and well-informed. We had to think about it, ponder it, and pray about it.

If you've lost some of that fire, don't worry. It happens to everyone in pretty much every endeavor. I had a lot of good, sound reasons for joining the Army at the age

of thirty-two. But about a week into Basic Training I couldn't remember a single one! But I was committed by then. I wasn't backing out.

And then six years later I switched branches to the Navy and entered the officer ranks. I had to do Basic all over again (more or less) in the form of Officer Indoctrination School. Not as hard physically, but more so mentally. The hours were just as long and the stress was just as high. And again, I found myself some days into it and wondering what I had gotten myself into. But again, I was committed, and had to move forward. So how did I? What did I do when the warning light came on?

What I found helpful (and still do) is getting back to my roots. Making sure those roots didn't skip across the stones and actually made it into the soil. Going back and listing all the reasons for what I do. Doing my best to remind myself why I'm here and why it's important. Reading my scriptures. Re-reading notes I took on blessings I've been given. Revisiting those reasons why *I* joined in the first place. Maintaining that open channel with God. And telling others, when the opportunity arises in a natural way, why I'm here. Like writing this book. A testimony gets stronger in the sharing of it.

And then we pick yourselves up and dust ourselves off and put our shoulders to the wheel again. And what happens? More obstacles arise. Trials weigh us down, sometimes worse than before. Doors are slammed on us. And we have another spell of doubt and have to go through all that building ourselves back up again. (And wash, rinse repeat!)

This is why baptism is not a checkbox on a form, but an entry to a path. That path may be straight but it's certainly not without its pitfalls (remember a few chapters ago what it said in Lehi's dream about mists of darkness and an iron rod). But as it says in Matthew 24:13, '... he that shall endure unto the end, the same shall be saved.'

So when that light comes on, handle it. Do your part *and* get the help you need. Remember Range Day! Don't cover it with electrical tape and keep going or you'll find yourself stuck in the hinterlands with no wheels and no cell service, relying on your own lonesome self to get out. Maybe you will, if you're resourceful enough. But you're going to deal with a lot of unnecessary suffering along the way and may have to leave behind things you'd rather not. I'd advise you to work smarter, not harder. (I first heard that one from Scrooge McDuck. You're welcome!)

With Great Power, Comes...?

'We have learned by sad experience that it is the nature and disposition of almost all men, as soon as they get a little authority, as they suppose, they will immediately begin to exercise unrighteous dominion.'

—Doctrine & Covenants 121:39

D ominion. A responsibility over something. The delegated authority to be 'in charge' of a task or operation, great or small, and make sure the job is done.

Why should we worry about dominion? Because we have been given it from the very start. According to the Books of Genesis, Moses and Abraham, man was to replenish the earth, subdue it, and have 'dominion' over every living thing. Must we exercise that dominion? No, of

course we have the option of not accepting a gift given us by God. He's not going to force us into heaven... but when we're standing before his judgement bar, he will ask us what we did with our lives, including our dominion. I'm pretty sure this is the meat in the parable of the Talents found in Matthew 25. When we are face to face with *our* Master, do we want to tell him we buried our dominion in the earth and did nothing with it?

For this reason, it behooves us to accept that gift and do the best we can with it. But what exactly is 'dominion'? All our sacrament talks (a.k.a. 'sermons') are given by the members of the congregation, who are asked some weeks in advance to prepare something on a particular topic. A lot of our speakers like to start off their talks with a dictionary definition, and while it can be a good start, I think it's risky to rely too much on Webster for religious clarity. Consider this: Webster lists definitions pretty much in order of prevalence—the first one is usually what most people think of when they are asked to define something. Webster's first definition for 'dominion' is:

> 'Dominance or power through legal authority,
> i.e., "the rule of Caesar"'.

But in comparison, 'prophet' has 'an authoritative person who *divines the future*'. I already addressed this in a previous chapter, but just to beat this horse completely to death: this shows that in the secular public view Moses is about on a par with Madame Zorko's Palm-Reading Emporium in Atlantic City. It is only in their Number 2 definition that anything shows up about 'inspired by God'.

So, when most people think about dominion they think of the 'rule of Caesar' (who was a total dictator, which is a nice, quick way to get yourself in trouble with those you're responsible for), but this is *not* what is meant by the dominion given us by God.

That dominion is a stewardship: we are given responsibility over a small part of the Kingdom of God, and it is our responsibility to see that it flourishes. What we are responsible for does not belong to us. If God owned a factory, we would be third-shift line foremen—able to act with some autonomy because the boss isn't on the floor, but not holding the power to sell the company forklift for a profit! We act with the boss's authority only so long as we do what the boss would have us do. This requires that we know the situation, the people involved, and the boss's mind, all pretty thoroughly.

We may be 'kings in our own houses', but according to Brigham Young, second president of the Church, 'a king's glory and success are measured by the happiness, prosperity, and increase of his subjects'. The noted LDS scholar Hugh Nibley explained it this way: '... the dominion God gives man is designed to test him, to enable him to show himself, his fellows, and all the heavens just how he would act if entrusted with God's own power...'

I didn't make a career out of the military, but thirteen years was long enough to give me fistfuls of analogies to use for things like this: Every unit has one CO, from the largest division to the smallest squad. This isn't to give the glory to that guy, because a successful CO knows when to hand out medals to his troops. Rather it is to know whom to hold accountable when things go wrong—and quite often it's the CO himself. As a matter of fact, it's part of an NCO's upbringing that anything that happens in their unit is their own fault. When things are done as a committee it's too easy to put the blame for mistakes on the other members and then we don't tend to work as hard as we can to make sure things are right.

Exercising *righteous* dominion—now that's the hard part. Why? Because we can't just react to a situation by

instinct. That's what animals do; they just react. It's their 'nature'. When we do the same, we are 'natural men', and according to both Romans 8:7 and Mosiah 3:19, 'the natural man is an enemy to God'. He gave us a brain and he expects us to use it (remember: 'study it out in your mind'). So when we are faced with challenges to our dominion, we can't just react. We need to think. And what we need to think about is 'what will accomplish the goal'.

If our goal is leading our family, if it's bringing up our children to love God, even if it's leading our little auxiliary group in the Church or heading up a work crew, this is not always necessarily the same as rigidly following rules. Remember that Jesus rebuked the Jewish leadership for taking observation of rules to a ridiculous level. They became so wrapped up in following the *letter* of the law they lost sight of the *spirit* of the law.

We are expected to keep the spirit of the law in mind, and this involves discernment. We are judges in our own sphere of responsibility, but being a judge does not mean being a blind enforcer. It means considering how the rules fit the situation. At times we may have to be willing to make a judgement call that might seem a little counter to the rules but is best in the long run for all involved *based on*

our best judgement, and *after a suitable amount of pondering* (remember what I said a while back about studying things out in your mind).

Here's a medical analogy: every medication on the market is approved by the FDA for certain diseases. But doctors are given the right to use medications for other conditions, what's called 'off-label' use, if in their best judgement it is appropriate. Mucomyst is a respiratory drug approved for reducing mucous in emphysema patients. It's also used widely (without FDA approval) for reducing kidney injury after having a CT scan with radioactive contrast dye—because it works. Doctors are given this privilege of off-label use because they have studied physiology, psychology, pharmacokinetics and so forth, and have a vested interest in the survival of the patient. We likewise have a vested interest in the success of our responsibilities. We may not have studied psychology and that other stuff to any great extent, but that is made up for by our access to God's intimate knowledge of each of us and our situations through that gift of the Holy Ghost I mentioned a while back.

However, we need to be mindful of our entitlement to judge when we exercise dominion. If we are lax, things

go awry, to be sure, but if we are too rigid, the people in our care rebel or become indifferent. It takes a sensitive hand on the controls. Sometimes exercising righteous dominion means upbraiding the unrighteous, like Abinadi did King Noah, and sometimes it means welcoming them with open arms like the Prodigal Son. Knowing where on that spectrum we need to be in our response to a given situation requires, as I said before, knowledge of the people, of the situation, and God's mind on these things. We need to exercise a 'Christlike love' for the people in our charge—we need to put ourselves in their shoes. We need to remember our own experiences when we were where they are. We need to know the situation by getting all the facts, and we need to live the gospel, and fast and pray if necessary, so that we can have access to the guidance of the Holy Ghost for those things about people and situations that we just can't know otherwise. And finally, we have to know God's will. We need to read the scriptures, attend church, ponder, pray, and we need to consult our leadership as the Spirit dictates.

In the LDS Church we believe that when our children reach the age of eight, in the eyes of God they are agents unto themselves and will thereafter be held accountable for their own actions. We are there to guide them: we encourage them when they do right, we express our

displeasure or disappointment when they do wrong, and as their parents we punish them if need be, but through it all we have to remember that we are supervising people who are children of God first and have been loaned to us, and that really we are only the ones 'with seniority'. Like camp counselors.

Consider the words of M. Russell Ballard, one of our apostles:

> 'These stewardships, equally sacred and important, do not involve any false ideas about domination or subordination. Each stewardship is essential for the spiritual progression of all family members, parents and children alike.'

God knows the burden he has given you. He knows that you are leading independent or strong-willed or even rebellious spirits. He knows because he has been doing the same for ages. If we recognize that we cannot force another down the path of righteousness, and can only ask God how best to proceed (and pay attention to the answers), we will do well.

Not What You're Built For

'Adam fell that men might be; and men are, that they might have joy.'

—2 Nephi 2:25

I mentioned back in the preface that this church makes sense to me. That as I investigated it, I started finding answers to questions I didn't know I had. One of these I touched on lightly I want to dig a little deeper into now:

Why the heck are we even here?

Back when I was still looking at churches and trying to figure out what the big attraction was, this was one of those things that seemed to be taken for granted but didn't make any sense: So you're telling me God made us, put us through all the horror, pain, and loss of this life, only to sort us into two boxes where we'll be left for all eternity? Where the ones that didn't respect him will face a never-ending sentence of whipping and burning, and the ones of

121

whom he approves will spend Forever doing... what? Telling him how great he is? Yeah, it wasn't an attractive proposition.

But what I found here was that there is much more to it than that. Much, much more. Now, bear with me: I'm not going to get into a lot of detail now as it's beyond the scope of what I'm trying to do. Kind of how God told Moses on Mount Sinai:

> 'And it came to pass, as the voice was still speaking, Moses cast his eyes and beheld the earth, yea, even all of it; and there was not a particle of it which he did not behold, discerning it by the Spirit of God.
> And he beheld also the inhabitants thereof, and there was not a soul which he beheld not; and he discerned them by the Spirit of God; and their numbers were great, even numberless as the sand upon the sea shore.
> And he beheld many lands; and each land was called earth, and there were inhabitants on the face thereof.
> And it came to pass that Moses called upon God, saying, Tell me, I pray thee, why these

things are so, and by what thou madest them? And behold, the glory of the Lord was upon Moses, so that Moses stood in the presence of God, and talked with him face to face. And the Lord God said unto Moses: For mine own purpose have I made these things....

And worlds without number have I created; and I also created them for mine own purpose...

But only an account of this earth, and the inhabitants thereof, give I unto you. For behold, there are many worlds that have passed away by the word of my power. And there are many that now stand, and innumerable are they unto man; but all things are numbered unto me, for they are mine and I know them.

And it came to pass that Moses spake unto the Lord, saying: Be merciful unto thy servant, O God, and tell me concerning this earth, and the inhabitants thereof, and also the heavens, and then thy servant will be content.'

—Moses 1:27-36

God has a job for us once we get to the other side. I mentioned earlier that he is going to need us to help manage the Universe. That's really an oversimplification, but we'll leave it there for now. I want to focus on what we're doing here, now. If your curiosity is getting the better of you then sit in on one of our services. You're welcome to just visit any time. If you're feeling adventurous you can talk to the missionaries. There's at least one pair assigned to every congregation, and they'll be embarrassingly excited to give you the whole rundown!

But as I said at the outset, *I'm* not trying to convert anyone. I'm just sharing what I've learned. We have an Article of Faith that says, 'we claim the privilege of worshipping Almighty God according to the dictates of our own conscience, and allow all men the same privilege, let them worship how, when or what they may'. So don't feel I'm trying to push our doctrine. I feel it just makes sense and explains a lot of things I didn't get before.

On the other hand, we also know that it is the responsibility of every man to warn his neighbor. It's not just the job of a prophet (remember what I said earlier about all of us being prophets in our own spheres?) and so we do what we can to let people know. We're not supposed

to be pushy about it, but also like I said before, the doctrine is perfect, but the church is made up of (and led by) imperfect people. In fact, all our leadership are rank amateurs! You don't get to be a ward bishop in the Church by having a theology degree. You get that calling because, for one reason or another, it's something you need to *learn* how to do. On-the-job training at its finest! Though it can make the first few years of any new bishop's term a little challenging for all involved! That's why when a new calling is issued, and accepted by the individual, it's put to the congregation for a sustaining vote. Not an *approving* vote, mind you. That person has already been selected for that job by divine call. What we raise our hands for is to confirm that we are willing to *sustain* that person as they try to learn the ropes. We will put up with their mistakes and help where we can.

It's been said, even amongst ourselves, that LDS folks tend to live in a bubble. That we only associate with others like us, to minimize the adverse influences of the world. That's very true because sometimes one can only take so much. But as the writer John Augustus Shedd once said:

'A ship in harbor is safe, but that is not what ships are built for'.

125

We didn't come here to play it safe (go back and read that parable of the talents), we came here (on our own volition, remember that Grand Council) to test ourselves. To see if we could learn God's lessons... one of which is loving your neighbor as yourself. Even if that neighbor is to you like Wednesday Addams was to Enid Sinclair! And when we graduate... I can't even begin to describe. I can't imagine the scale of it all.

But like all tests, life is difficult. Even overwhelming. I want you to know that you *do* have a purpose here, to prepare yourself for what God has planned for us after, and he *does* want you to succeed. We may not have been built for staying safe in harbor, but neither were we made just to dash ourselves upon the reefs. Some of us may sail recklessly and bring our doom upon ourselves but even the most careful mariner can get caught by a rogue wave or a shifting sandbar. But keep a couple things in mind: first, God's own stated mission:

> 'For behold, this is my work and my glory—to bring about the immortality and eternal life of man.'
>
> —Moses 1:39

And one of my personal favorites, how all this is temporary:

> '... I will restore to you the years that the locust hath eaten, the cankerworm, and the palmerworm, my great army which I sent among you.'
>
> —Joel 2:25

Life is rough. Painful. Scary. Often unjust. But it has a purpose beyond just being sorted into boxes and forgotten. Realize it or not, you are a child of a God who needs you. You were made to come here, experience life, and learn from it. Not to stay in a harbor, safely tethered to the pier, but likewise not to just sail over the edge.

You were built to meet your greatest potential.

About The Author

Steve grew up on a farm in Northeast Ohio, then worked in factories for fifteen years before going back to school and becoming a physician. His other writing ventures have been novels, and he has won awards for his writing in collaboration with Michael Eging on *The Silver Horn Echoes: A Song of Roland*, and *The Paladin of Shadow Chronicles: Book One, Annwyn's Blood*, and *Book Two: Ash and Ruin.*

also available **TAYLOR & WELLS**
from

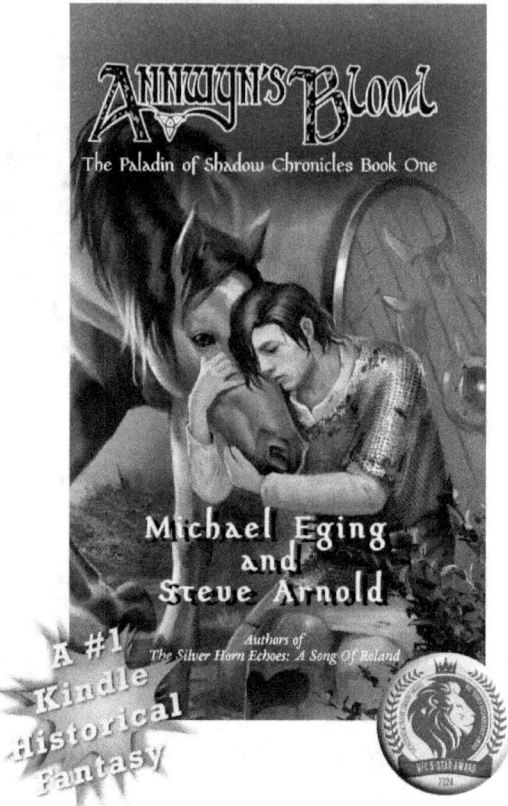

"*A fantastic read... its pacing is perfect, the characterization intuitive, and the style is perfect for the dark setting.*"
Stuart Kenyon, author of the *Augmented* series

Available now on
amazon

www.ingramcontent.com/pod-product-compliance
Lightning Source LLC
Chambersburg PA
CBHW060539130626
46553CB00002B/822